SMART IZOD

Finance & Accounting
cases and problems

Calculating BEP — 94 95 96 97
Limiting resources — 101 102
Investment Appraisal — 139 148 149
                   Payback WACC

MC — AC   — 107 108 109

Finance in Organisations

Humphrey Shaw

An introduction, for the not-so-numerate, to the financial aspects of
management in organisations. With diagrams, charts, company accounts &
clear explanations, the reader is guided through the main methods of
understanding and controlling the finances of a business.
Book - £10.95 (large format paperback), isbn 1 85450 019 8
Tutor's Manual of worked exercises (suitable for class use or as a free-
standing 2-day short course for managers new to the subject) - £59.00 (free
with 15+ books bought direct)   isbn 1 85450 031 7
Projection Pack of 44 overhead projection transparencies to support the book
and the Tutor's Manual - £59.00   isbn 1 85450 037 6

A Manager's Guide to **Quantitative Methods** - 2nd edition

Michael Cuming

Updated, revised and with a completely new chapter on Getting Things done
on Time. This popular textbook is used on DMS, HNC/D and other
introductory level courses for business and professional students.
One of the most-appreciated features of the book is its appeal to not-so-
numerate people as it leads with a business or work problem, gradually
introducing the numerical and statistical methods to solve it.
Contents include:
Frequency distributions; Getting the right answer from your calculator;
Summarising distributions; The language of uncertainty; Compound interest
and discounting; Correlation and regression - a statistical minefield; Tracking
things in time; Finding out by sampling; Drawing conclusions; Managing with
the computer; Problems with data; Getting things done on time.

£11.95   isbn 1 85450 021 X   544 pages   Paperback

Finance & Accounting
cases and problems

Humphrey Shaw

ELM Publications

ISBN 1 85450 087 2

CONTENTS

Dedication   ix
Acknowledgements   x
Introduction   xi
About the Author   xii

QUESTIONS, EXERCISES & CASE STUDIES

1	Case Study - Tube Masters	1
2-3	Cash book entries	2
4	Debiting/crediting accounts	3
5	Debiting/crediting accounts	4
6	Recording cash transactions	5
7	Recording in the ledgers	6
8	Trial balance	7
9	Case Study - The Tool Box	8
10	Assets or liabilities	9
11	Assets or liabilities	10
12	Assets or liabilities	11
13-18	Calculating capital	12-13
19	Completing balance sheet figures	14
20	Net assets	15
21	Completing balance sheet figures	16
22-24	Capital and revenue expenditure	17-19
25-31	Entering transactions into accounts	20-26
32-37	Calculate gross profit	27-28
38	Accounting terminology	29
39	Case Study - The Confectionery Store	30
40	Case Study - The Flower Shop	31
41	Case Study - New Ventures	32
42	Case Study - Mountain Biker	33
43	Case Study - Gardens and Lawns	34
44	Case Study - Master Crafts	35
45	Case Study - Travel There	36
46	Case Study - Hutton's Shoe Shop	37
47	Case Study - Harry's Pet Shop	38
48	Case Study - Electrical Wholesalers Limited	39
49	Case Study - Spark of Life Limited	40
50	Recording information/Companies' Act, 1985	41

51	Case Study - The General Trading Company Ltd	42
52	Case Study - Plumbing Supplies Limited	43
53	Executive Stationery Supplies	44
54	Case Study - Road Hauliers	45
55-65	Valuing assets/depreciation	46-48
66	Case Study - European Hauliers	49
67	Case Study - Plant Hire	50
68	Case Study - Zolan Limited	51
69	Case Study - Zoraq Limited	52
70	Case Study - Markan Limited	53
71	Case Study - The Electric Motor Cmpany	54
72-84	Calculating costs/contribution	55-58
85-87	Calculating break even/margin of safety	59
88-89	Product decisions	60
90	Case Study - Monal Limited	61
91	Case Study - Trees and Shrubs	62
92	Case Study - Adventure Parks Limited	63
93	Case Study - Harvest Pies	64
94	Case Study - Hi Slope Skis	65
95	Case Study - Bridge Hotel	66
96	Case Study - Leaded Lights	67
97	Case Study - Geoff's Garage	68
98	Case Study - Watch Straps	69
99	Case Study - Down at Heel	70
100	Case Study - The Potter's Wheel	71
101	Case Study - Tailored Suits	72
102	Case Study - River Craft	73
103	Case Study - Smithdown Stores	74
104	Case Study - Metal Forge Masters	75
105	Case Study - Carpets and Curtains	76
106	Case Study - Southern Cross Hotel	77
107	Case Study - Central Theme Parks	78
108	Case Study - Leather Crafts	79
109	Case Study - Leisure Cruises	80
110	Case Study - The South West Brewing Company	81
111	Case Study - The Wooden Fencing Company	82
112	Case Study - R & H Metal Manufacturers	83
113	Case Study - The Malaysian Restaurant	84
114	Material usage variances	85
115	Direct labour variances	86
116	Material price variances	87

117	Case Study - Executive Traveller	88
118	Case Study - The Kitchen Mouldings Company	89
119	Case Study - Irons and Woods	90
120	Case Study - The Welsh Honey Farm	91
121	Case Study - The Woollen Rug Company	92
122	Case Study - Leather Boots Limited	93-94
123	Case Study - The Griffin Paint Company	95-96
124-126	Source/Application of funds	97-99
127	Case Study - The Rose Garden Nursery	100
128	Case Study - The Pattisserie	101
129	Case Study - The Whole Wheat Bakery	102
130	Case Study - Acquarians Limited	103
131	Case Study - Barton Lodge Crafts	104
132	Ratios and what they measure	105
133	Case Study - The Diverse Engineering Group	106
134	Case Study - Transic PLC	107
135	Case Study - The Takeover Battle	108-109
136	Case Study - Harlequin Tours	110
137	Case Study - The Wine Grotto	111-112
138-139	Pay back times	113-114
140-141	Accounting rate of return	115
142-145	Net present value/return on investment	116-117
146	Case Study - Steel Stockholders Limited	118
147	Case Study - Wood Supplies	119
148	Case Study - The Village Lawn Tennis Club	120
149	Case Study - Mountain Tours	121
150	Case Study - Travel Tours	122

SUGGESTED ANSWERS (numerical order, as above) 123-206

APPENDICES

Glossary of Financial Terms	*207-213*
The Key Accounting Ratios	*214-216*
DCF Tables	*217*
Present Value of £1 Tables	*218-219*
Prescribed Formats for Company Accounts	
Balance Sheet - Format 1	*220-221*
Profit and Loss account - Format 1	*222*
Profit and Loss Account - Format 2	*222-223*

DEDICATION

To my Grandparents, Phoebe and Robert Rudkin.

ACKNOWLEDGEMENTS

Thank you to all the people who helped in the production of this book:

At the University of North London - Ishbel MacDonald, Helen Payne, Denise Naylor and Mark Inman.

At the University of Surrey - Sally Messenger.

At West Herts College - Helena Shaw and Tony Head.

Introduction

More and more management writers are stressing the importance of information as one of the key corporate resources. Today's managers are part of this information age, needing accurate data if they are to be able to plan, to make decisions and to control the organisation's activities.

One of the main sources of information in any business is the vast amount of data generated by the accounting function which, if the manager is to make better decisions must be understood. Once armed with this knowledge, the manager is better able to control their orgainsation from both an operational and strategic standpoint.

Many people studying finance for the first time find it a difficult subject. There is not just a new vocabulary to learn but also one must know the correct layout for presenting financial information, whilst at the same time making all the correct calculations.

The key to understanding finance is practice. This book covers the main topics which are generally included on any course in finance. Each question builds on the last so that the more difficult concepts are only introduced once the basics have been mastered. At the back of the book you will find suggested answers to all of the questions, together with helpful notes which explain where appropriate how the figures have been calculated. There is also a Glossary of Financial Terms, together with the correct layout as prescribed by the Companies' Act for final accounts.

Humphrey Shaw, June, 1992.

ABOUT THE AUTHOR

Humphrey Shaw is a Senior Lecturer in Finance and accounting at the University of North London.

Question 1

Tube Masters

The Finance Department has always been situated in the basement at Tubemasters. The company specalises in making metal tubing and its products are used mainly in the food processing industry. Most people in the company have no idea what goes on in the finance office except that periodically they have to go there for petty cash receipts or to see the management accountant when the annual budgets are prepared.

The Head of Public Relations has decided to run a feature on the work done by the Finance Department in the company magazine. The Editor has looked at the firm's organisation chart (which is shown below) but is not certain why the firm employs three functional heads to look after its finances.

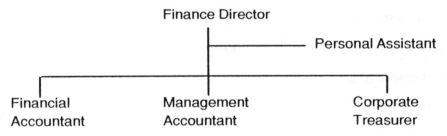

Unfortunately the chart does not contain any additional information and so the Editor has decided to send a memo to the Finance Director requesting information on the work carried out by each specalist function under her control. You work as the Finance Director's Personal Assistant and have been asked to draft a reply to the memo from the Public Relations Department.

Question 2

Write up the cash book to record the following cash transactions of a small market trader and balance the account for the 10th of February Year 7.

February		£
1	Opening balance	100
2	Bought stamps	20
3	Cash sales	10
4	Paid rent	15
5	Paid wages	20
6	Bought petrol for van	12
7	Bought office stationery	5
8	Cash sales	30
9	Paid cash into bank	15
10	Cash sales	25

Question 3

Balance the Cash Book from the information given below:

Cash Book

	£		£
Opening Balance	100	Stationery	20
Cash Sales	50	Stamps	30

Question 4

Using the spaces provided, write down which account is to be debited and which account should be credited.

	Transaction	Debit	Credit
a	Opened a business bank account with cash		
b	Bought stationery by cheque		
c	Bought stock by cash		
d	Sold stock and received payment in cash		
e	Bought motor van paid by cheque		
f	Bought stock by cheque		
g	Bought petrol for van with cash		
h	Withdrew cash from the business		
i	Sold goods on credit to R Khan		
j	Paid insurance by cheque		
k	Paid rent by cheque		

Question 5

Using the spaces provided, write down which account should be debited and credited.

	Transaction	Debit	Credit
a	Started a business with £1,000 in cash		
b	Opened a business bank account with £500 cash.		
c	Bought stock for £300. Paid by cheque.		
d	Sold some stock for £200 and was paid in cash.		
e	Bought a business computer for £600 paid by cheque.		
f	Sold some stock for £100 received cheque.		
g	Bought stationery for £50 cash		
h	Paid £500 cash into the business		
i	Withdrew £30 from the business bank A/C		
j	Paid cleaner £5 in cash		

Question 6

Record the following cash transactions for a small factory canteen in the appropriate Ledger Account.

Week One

		£
Day 1	Opening balance	80.00
	Purchases	40.00
	Sales	60.00
	Cash paid into bank	10.00
Day 2	Purchases	30.00
	Milk Bill	12.60
	Cleaning materials	4.30
	Sales	40.00
Day 3	Purchases	50.00
	Sales	90.00
	Gas Bill	27.30
Day 4	Purchases	45.00
	Sales	70.00
	Laundry	15.00
	Cash paid into bank	12.00
Day 5	Purchases	30.00
	Sales	45.00
	Wages	60.00
	Cash paid into bank	20.00

Question 7

Complete the following table by stating the type of account which has been affected by the transaction and how it should be recorded in the ledgers. An example is shown below:

	Transaction	Ledgers	Account	Dr/Cr.
a	Bought Office Computer paid cash	Computer Cash	Real Real	Debit Credit
b	Paid £50 cash into bank account			
c	Bought stock on credit from GH Ltd			
d	Paid wages by writing a cheque			
e	Bought new premises paid by cheque			
f	Sold goods for cash to D Patel			
g	Paid telephone bill with cash			
h	Bought office computer on credit from KL Supplies			
i	Sold goods on credit to H Ltd			
j	Bought stock paid cash			
k	Withdrew £30 cash from bank account			
l	Paid insurance by cheque			
m	Sold office typewriter for cash			

6

Question 8

In a trial balance, state whether the following balances would be shown as debits or credits.

	Transaction	Debit	Credit
a	Sales		
b	Commission Received		
c	Motor Vehicles		
d	Opening Stock		
e	Provision for Depreciation		
f	Bank Loan		
g	Freehold Premises		
h	Purchases		
i	Drawings		
j	Office Furniture		
k	Insurance		
l	Cash		
m	Carriage Inwards		
n	Carriage Outwards		
o	Office Wages		
p	Warehouse Wages		
q	Debtors		
r	Returns Inwards		
s	Returns Outwards		
t	Rent and Rates		
u	Debenture		
v	Plant and Machinery		
w	Light and Heating		
x	Telephone Charges		
y	Motor Vehicle Repairs		
z	Capital		

Question 9

The Tool Box

Brian Hawkins has been in business for one year selling a range of hand tools. Unfortunately he has not kept a record of the amount of money which he has invested in the business. He has extracted a list of ledger balances but has sent them to you because they do not balance. Using the information below, draw up the firm's Trial Balance for the 5 April, Year One and calculate its capital.

	£
Sales	45,890
Commission Received	1,540
Freehold Premises	73,000
Purchases	22,583
Motor Van	800
Heat and Light	300
Wages	7,000
Carriage Inwards	200
Office Cleaning	340
Rent and Rates	1,350
Discount Received	400
Discount Allowed	230
Fixtures and Fittings	2,560
Debtors	8,300
Creditors	22,000
Bank Loan	1,500
Motor Expenses	400
Returns Inwards	100
Capital	?

Question 10

State which of the following would be shown as assets or liabilities in a balance sheet.

		Asset	Liability
a	Closing Stock		
b	Taxation		
c	Debentures		
d	Work in Progress		
e	Bill of Exchange Payable		
f	Shares in Group Companies		
g	Patents		
h	Accruals		
i	Company Car		
j	Bank Overdraft		
k	Carpet and Curtains		
l	Debtors		
m	Secured Loan		
n	Licence		
o	Reserves		
p	Retained Profit		
q	Ski Lift		
r	Government Gilts		
s	Share Capitol		
t	Preference Shares		

Question 11

State which of the following would be shown as assets or liabilities in a balance sheet.

		Asset	Liability
a	Fixtures and Fittings		
b	Bank Overdraft		
c	Cash		
d	Money owed to a supplier		
e	Rent prepayment		
f	Capital		
g	Motor Vehicles		
h	Plant and Machinery		
i	Office Computer		
j	Creditors		
k	Bank Balance		
l	Bank Loan		
m	Development Costs		
n	Loan from friend		
o	Leasehold Property		
p	Goodwill		
q	Investments		
r	Mortgage		

Question 12

State which of the following would be shown as assets or liabilities in a company balance sheet.

		Asset	Liability
a	Debenture		
b	Shares in subsidiary		
c	Patent		
d	Share Premium		
e	Development Costs		
f	Amounts owed to Group Companies		
g	Capital Redemption Reserve		
h	Goodwill		
i	Ordinary Share Capital		
j	Loans to Related Companies		
k	Fixtures and Fittings		
l	Deferred Income		
m	Plant and Machinery		
n	Licences		
o	Work in Progress		
p	Investments		
q	Bank Loans		
r	Called up Capital		
s	Payments on Account		
t	Profit and Loss Account		

Question 13

Calculate the firm's capital from the following information:

a)	Fixed Assets	£23,500	Capital	?
b)	Total Assets	£16,430	Capital	?
c)	Net Assets	£56,740	Capital	?

Question 14

Calculate the capital and total assets for the following different firms from the information given below:

		£ Yr1	£ Yr2	£ Yr3	£ Yr4
a)	Fixed Assets	17,500	5,430	8,460	34,790
b)	Current Assets	5,000	800	2,540	12,543
c)	Total Assets	?	?	?	?
d)	Capital	?	?	?	?

Question 15

Calculate the capital and net assets for the following different firms from the information given below:

		£ Yr1	£ Yr2	£ Yr3	£ Yr4
a)	Fixed Assets	12,000	34,000	7,600	21,600
b)	Current Assets	3,400	5,700	1,430	3,900
c)	Current Liabilities	2,900	3,780	400	876
d)	Net Assets	?	?	?	?
e)	Capital	?	?	?	?

Question 16

a) During the last four years a company has had the following retained profits. The owner's initial investment in the business was £10,000. Calculate the firm's capital for each of the last four years.

	Year 1 £	Year 2 £	Year 3 £	Year 4 £
Retained Profit	3,560	4,579	7,520	8.520

Question 17

b) Five years ago Mr Napier started a business with £20,000. Each year the business has been profitable and he has taken drawings out . From the information given below, calculate the capital of the firm for each of the last four years.

	Year 1 £	Year 2 £	Year 3 £	Year 4 £
Profit	12,400	8,509	9.786	15,763
Drawings	3,100	4,600	4,794	6,609
Capital	?	?	?	?

Question 18

c) Calculate the firm's capital from the following information:

	Year 1 £	Year 2 £	Year 3 £	Year 4 £
Assets	15,000	16,700	18,400	22,560
Current Liabilities	3,400	4,670	5,450	8,900
Capital	?	?	?	?

13

Question 19

From the following information calculate the missing figure.

	Capital £	Current Liabilities £	Fixed Assets £	Current Assets £
a	25,000	15,000	30,000	?
b	?	30,000	40,000	20,000
c	15,000	?	40,000	15,000
d	70,000	45,000	90,000	?
e	27,000	14,000	?	10,000
f	60,000	?	80,000	30,000
g	?	28,000	45,000	29,000
h	75,000	40,000	76,000	?
i	50,000	23,000	?	33,000
j	45,000	18,000	30,000	?

14

Question 20

From the following information calculate the net assets of the business.

	Capital £	Current Liabilities £	Fixed Assets £	Current Assets £	Net Assets £
a	40,000	20,000	35,000	25,000	?
b	70,000	45,000	60,000	55,000	?
c	25,000	15,000	17,000	23,000	?
d	80,000	22,000	50,000	?	?
e	?	40,000	63,000	50,000	?
f	45,000	30,000	?	35,000	?
g	54,000	?	70,000	22,000	?
h	90,000	30,000	?	35,000	?
i	?	25,000	40,000	33,000	?
j	46,000	?	34,000	25,000	?

15

Question 21

Complete the following table:

	Capital	Current Liabilities	Fixed Assets	Current Assets	Working Capital
	£	£	£	£	£
a	40,000	20,000	30,000	?	?
b	?	35,000	28,000	32,000	?
c	40,000	?	30,000	15,000	?
d	?	15,000	60,000	40,000	?
e	35,000	10,000	?	?	12,000
f	?	20,000	15,000	10,000	?
g	70,000	?	67,000	14,000	?
h	45,000	18,000	23,000	?	?
i	?	?	50,000	35,000	20,000

16

Question 22

Give three examples of capital and revenue expenditure for the following four different types of business

HOTEL	Capital	Revenue
1		
2		
3		

SPORTS CENTRE	Capital	Revenue
1		
2		
3		

LEISURE PARK	Capital	Revenue
1		
2		
3		

CAR FACTORY	Capital	Revenue
1		
2		
3		

Question 23

Which of the following would be shown as capital and which as revenue expenditure?

		Capital Expenditure	Revenue Expenditure
a	Wages		
b	Purchase of Motor Vehicle		
c	Office Cleaning		
d	Factory Extension		
e	Spare Replacement Engine		
f	Survey fee for purchase of new office		
g	Heating and Lighting		
h	Depreciation of fixed assets		
i	Postage and Telephone		
j	Leasehold Premises		
k	Office Carpet		
l	Insurance		
m	Goodwill		

Question 24

State whether the following expenditure would be shown as revenue or capital expenditure in a firm's final accounts.

a) Purchase of a word processor

b) Solicitor's fee for conveyance of new property

c) Hire of a cement mixer

d) Painting the firm's logo on a new van

e) Purchase of royalty rights

f) Factory labour used in preparation of a new shed

g) Purchase of a lap top computer

h) Cost of sending an employee on a training course

i) Fitting a replacement monitor to the firm's desk top computer

j) Delivery cost of a new machine tool purchased by the firm.

k) Leasing payments for director's car

l) Purchase of new desks for secretaries

m) Payment of yearly window cleaning contract

n) Installation cost of new burglar alarm

o) Development costs of new product

p) Promotional cost of advertising the firm's products

r) Purchase of leasehold premises with 999 years title remaining

s) Installation costs of new computer system

Question 25

Record the following items under the appropriate heading:

	Transaction	Asset	Liability	Expense
a	Wages			
b	Motor Vehicles			
c	Debentures			
d	Rent			
e	Postage			
f	Computer			
g	Debtors			
h	Depreciation			
i	Creditors			
j	Premises			
k	Fixtures and Fittings			
l	Closing Stock			
m	Printing and Stationery			
n	Bank Overdraft			
o	Office Cleaning			
p	Work in Progress			
q	Debentures			
r	Share Capital			
s	Insurance			
t	Accruals			
u	Tax Payable			

Question 26

Using the spaces provided, state in which end of year financial statement the following transactions should be recorded:

	Transaction	Trading Account	Profit and Loss
a	Sales		
b	Warehouse Wages		
c	Carriage Outwards		
d	Discount Received		
e	Rent and Rates		
f	Light and Heating		
g	Opening Stock		
h	Carriage Inwards		
i	Discount Allowed		
j	Returns Inwards		
k	Rent Received		
l	Motor expenses		
m	Purchases		
n	Postage		
o	Telephone		
p	Closing Stock		
q	Commission Received		
r	Rent Received		

Question 27

State in which account the following information would be shown:

	Transaction	Trading Account	Profit and Loss
a	Returns Outwards		
b	Carriage Inwards		
c	Sales		
d	Closing Stock		
e	Insurance		
f	Warehouse Wages		
g	Purchases		
h	Heating and Lighting		
i	Wages		
j	Discount Received		
k	Carriage Outwards		
l	Depreciation		
m	Discount Allowed		
n	Postage and Telephone		
o	Rent Received		
p	Bank Charges		
q	Rent and Rates		
r	Motor Expenses		

Question 28

In which account would you expect to find the following information?

	Transaction	Trading Account	Profit & Loss
a	Sales		
b	Carriage Outwards		
c	Purchases		
d	Wages		
e	Returns Outwards		
f	Depreciation		
g	Heating and Lighting		
h	Postage and Stationery		
i	Closing Stock		
j	Discount Received		
k	Commission Received		
l	Interest Payments		
m	Returns Inwards		
n	Rent and Rates		
o	Insurance Payments		
p	Bad Debts		
q	Carriage Inwards		
r	Interest Received		
s	Commission Paid		

Question 29

In which account would you expect to find the following information?

	Transaction	Income	Expense	Asset	Liability
a	Commission Received				
b	Rent				
c	Bank Overdraft				
d	Discount Allowed				
e	Premises				
f	Sales				
g	Interest Received				
h	Wages				
i	Debtors				
j	Insurance				
k	Secured Loan				
l	Carriage Outwards				
m	Discount Received				
n	Laundry Expenses				
o	Interest Payments				
p	Heating and Electricity				
q	Creditors				
r	Cash				
s	Motor Van				
t	Fixtures and Fittings				
u	Discount Received				

Question 30

In which account or accounts would you expect to find the following information?

	Transaction	Trading Account	Profit & Loss	Balance Sheet
a	Debtors			
b	Opening Stock			
c	Heating and Lighting			
d	Depreciation Provision			
e	Ceditors			
f	Carriage Inwards			
g	Discount Received			
h	Share Capital			
i	Debentures			
j	Drawings			
k	Purchases			
l	Closing Stock			
m	Carriage Outwards			
n	Returns Inwards			
o	Lap Top Computer			
p	Postage and Telephone			
q	Cash			
r	Bank Overdraft			
s	Premises			
t	Unsecured Loan			
u	Discount Allowed			

Question 31

In which account would the following items be found in a firm's set of annual accounts?

	Transaction	Trading Account	Profit & Loss	Balance Sheet
a	Opening Stock			
b	Wages			
c	Lighting			
d	Heating			
e	Motor Vehicle			
f	Repairs to Motor Vehicle			
g	Premises			
h	Rent			
i	Rates			
j	Creditors			
k	Bank overdraft			
l	Cash			
m	Postage and Telephone			
n	Debtors			
o	Sales			
p	Capital			
q	Office Computer			
r	Drawings			
s	Office Stationery			

Question 32

From the following information, calculate the firm's gross profit:

	£ Year 1	£ Year 2	£ Year 3	£ Year 4
Sales	34,000	50,900	28,400	66,900
Purchases	14,500	27,400	13,568	34,810
Gross Profit	?	?	?	?

Question 33

From the following information, calculate the firm's gross profit:

	£ Year 1	£ Year 2	£ Year 3	£ Year 4
Sales	23,720	88,921	82,076	29,491
Cost of Goods Sold	15,840	46,820	38,491	5,930
Gross Profit	?	?	?	?

Question 34

From the following information, calculate the firm's gross profit:

	£
Sales	36,700
Purchases	23,800
Opening Stock	5,832
Closing stock	3,100

Question 35

From the following information, calculate the firm's gross profit:

	£
Returns Inwards	750
Carriage Inwards	430
Sales	25,100
Purchases	11,400
Opening stock	2,300
Closing Stock	1,500

Question 36

From the following information, calculate the firm's gross profit:

	£
Sales	65,700
Closing Stock	4,567
Returns Outwards	3,200
Carriage Inwards	1,398
Purchases	22,490
Opening Stock	7,420

Question 37

From the following information calculate the firm's net profit:

	£
Gross Profit	23,500
Rent	500
Wages	2,000
Insurance	700
Discount Received	300
Telephone and Postage	800
Depreciation	900

Question 38

What is the correct accounting terminology to describe the following transactions?

	Transaction	Accounting Terminology
a	Withdrew savings to form a business	
b	Sold goods on credit to a customer	
c	Paid to have purchases delivered	
d	Reduced customer's bill by 2% for early payment	
e	Returned defective purchases to supplier	
f	Bought stock on credit from Warehouses Ltd.	
g	Paid rent six months in advance	
h	Paid £97 instead of £100 because of prompt payment	
i	Paid to have goods delivered to customer	
j	Stock of partly made goods in factory	

Question 39

The Confectionery Store

Last year Mr Kennedy decided to start a small business. He bought the lease on a shop and stocked it with a range of confectionery, soft drinks and other inexpensive consumer items. During the first year he has been very busy because, as well as running the shop, he has continued working on the night shift at a local factory. This has helped him earn extra money but, unfortunately, he has not kept separate ledger accounts showing all of the firm's financial transactions.

Mr Kennedy needs to know how much money he has invested in the business. He knows that the shop lease cost £17,000, which he paid by withdrawing that sum from his building society account. On searching through his paper work, you have been able to ascertain the following information for the last day of the financial year one. This is summarised below:

	£
Delivery Van	4,000
Closing Stock	18,000
Bank Loan	3,000
Debtors	500
Creditors	3,000
Cash	8,000

You have been asked to prepare an accounting statement to show the amount of capital which Mr Kennedy has invested in the business during the last financial year.

Question 40

The Flower Shop

Rosemary Oakley has been in business for a year. She has just received her accounts and is worried that her assets only equal her liabilities. She has just shown you a copy of her latest balance sheet.

The Flower Shop as at 5th April, Year One.
Year One

Capital	£	Fixed Assets	£
Owner's Equity	20,000	Premises	10,000
Profits	7,000	Fixtures and Fittings	5,000
	27,000	Motor Vehicles	4,000
Drawings	4,000		
	23,000		19,000

Current Liabilities		Current Assets	
Creditors	5,000	Stock	2,000
		Debtors	4,000
		Bank	2,500
		Cash	500
	28,000		28,000

Redraft her balance sheet to show the firm's net assets, by preparing the balance sheet in vertical format, and write a memo explaining why a firm's assets must always equal its liabilities.

Question 41

New Ventures

Simon Mahoney has been in business for one year selling a range of household furnishings from an industrial unit, under the brand name New Ventures. He has just received the following information from his accountant.

	Dr £	Cr £
Capital		36,000
Drawings	15,000	
Profit and Loss Account		17,700
Debtors	19,260	
Creditors		25,860
Bank Term Loan		6,000
Stock	28,020	
Premises	12,060	
Cash at Bank	11,220	
	85,560	85,560

Simon needs to know:

a) the firm's fixed assets

b) the firm's working capital

c) the net assets of the business

d) the firm's capital employed

Question 42

Mountain Biker

Mr Killick set up Mountain Biker this year and has just finished his first year of trading. He has asked you to prepare his Trading and Profit And Loss account for the year ending 31 March, Year One.

Trial Balance for the year ending 31 March Year One		
	Dr	Cr
	£	£
Sales		60,000
Purchases	35,500	
Closing Stock	7,000	
Wages	10,000	
Light and Heating	3,000	
Postage and Telephone	1,500	
Cleaning	1,000	
Motor expenses	700	
Repairs to shop	500	
General Expenses	800	
	60,000	60,000

Question 43

Gardens and Lawns

John Mahoney is a landscape gardener and has just finished his first year in business. He is anxious to know whether or not he has made a profit and has asked you to prepare his Trading, Profit and Loss and Balance Sheet for the year ending 5 April Year One.

	Dr	Cr
	£	£
Sales		101,160
Purchases	54,225	
Wages	31,230	
Office Expenses	4,410	
Motor Expenses	2,565	
Office Cleaning	855	
Advertising	2,025	
Insurance	1,125	
Capital		20,000
Bank Overdraft		7,000
Creditors		14,445
Debtors	46,170	
	142,605	142,605

Closing stock at the year end was valued at £13,275

Question 44

Master Crafts

Master Crafts is the name given to a small business which operates in a local market in Hertfordshire selling artist's materials. The business is managed by Rachel Grant. The firm has just completed its year end and Rachel has asked you to prepare her firm's Trading and Profit and Loss Account and the Balance Sheet for the year ending 31 March, Year 8.

	Dr	Cr
	£	£
Sales		56,200
Opening Stock	8,150	
Purchases	21,000	
Carriage Inwards	975	
Wages	17,350	
Advertising	2,000	
Carriage Outwards	175	
Capital		10,000
Bank Term Loan		5,000
Rent	3,925	
Creditors		8,025
Debtors	19,425	
Cash at Bank	6,225	
	79,225	79,225

At the year end Rachel had closing stock of £7,375

Notes:

Rent Prepaid £300

Question 45

Travel There

The directors of Travel There have just completed their first twelve months of trading and are anxious to know whether or not the business has made a profit. The ledgers have all been balanced and the following balances extracted for the year ending 5 April, Year One:

	£	£
Commission Income		38,765
Bank Interest Paid	130	
Rent	9,768	
Wages	20,916	
Heating	876	
Office Stationery	300	
Office Sundries	100	
Postage	2,739	
Telephone	76	
Travelling Expenses	580	
Leasing Payments	450	
Discount Received		450
Discount Allowed	880	
Cleaning	2,400	
	39,215	39,215

The directors have asked you to prepare their firm's profit and loss account.

Notes:

Wages owing £100

Leasing Payments paid in Advance £120

Question 46

Hutton's Shoe Shop

Andrea Hutton has just completed her first year's trading and has drawn up her trial balance as at 5 April, Year Two. She would like to know the firm's profit or loss for the year, together with a statement showing the firm's assets and liabilities. She has asked you to prepare the firm's Profit and Loss account and Balance sheet from the following information.

	Dr	Cr
	£	£
Opening Stock	12,996	
Sales	8,600	73,848
Wages	45,520	
Purchases	10,600	
Lighting and Heating	444	
Insurance	420	
General Expenses	4,800	
Fixtures and Fittings	7,800	
Debtors		6,152
Creditors	4,000	
Cash	6,356	
Drawings		3,840
Bank Loan		17,696
Capital	101,536	101,536

Closing stock £10,192

Note:

Lighting and Heating Owing £150

General Expenses Prepaid £50

37

Question 47

Harry's Pet Shop

From the information given below, prepare the firm's Profit and Loss account and the Balance sheet for the year ending 31 December, Year Four.

	Dr	Cr
	£	£
Opening Stock	32,490	
Sales		187,320
Bank Overdraft		2,300
Wages	21,500	
Purchases	113,800	
Returns Inwards	2,700	
Lighting and Heating	26,500	
Carriage Outwards	6,000	
Motor Repairs	1,110	
Loan		3,000
Sundry Expenses	1,050	
Motor Vehicles	12,000	
Debtors	19,500	
Creditors		18,380
Cash	10,500	
Drawings	15,390	
Bank Loan		12,600
Capital		38,940
	262,540	262,540

Closing stock £25,480

38

Question 48

Electrical Wholesalers Limited

You work in the Accounts Department and have been asked to prepare the company's balance sheet for the year ending 5th April, Year 7 from the following information.

	£
Freehold Premises	296,000
Furniture and Fittings	95,830
Motor Vehicles	32,560
Stock	68,450
Debtors	59,200
Goodwill	20,000
General Reserve	5,000
Share Premium	15,000
Bank Balance	12,950
Creditors	109,990
Debenture	155,000
300,000 £1 Ordinary Shares Issued and fully paid	300,000

Question 49

Spark of Life Limited

The company specalise in fitting discounted car and lorry batteries. The firm has just finished its half year of trading and has asked you to prepare its Trading, Profit and Loss Account and the Balance Sheet for the half year ending 31 September, Year Five.

	£	£
70,000 Ord £1 Shares Issued and fully paid		70,000
Purchases	113,602	
Insurance	27,356	
Sales		189,423
Carriage Inwards	8,901	
Carriage Outwards	3,402	
Discount Allowed	3,954	
Commission Received		2,702
Goodwill	25,000	
Revaluation Reserve		15,000
General Reserve		10,000
Wages	20,630	
Directors' Emoluments	15,201	
Advertising	3,200	
Rent and Rates	11,982	
Debtors	10,707	
Creditors		6,037
Cash at Bank	13,920	
Investments	4,000	
Motor Vehicles	16,520	
Opening Stock	14,787	
	293,162	293,162

At the year end, the firm had closing stock which was valued at £20,045.

Question 50

In a con... any balance sheet prepared for publication how should the following information be recorded so that it complies with the 1985 Companies' Act?

a) Shares in group companies

b) Development Costs

c) Called up share capital not paid

d) Goodwill

e) Debenture Loans

f) Loans to related companies

g) Profit and Loss Account

h) Plant and machinery

i) Work in progress

j) Trade creditors

k) Patents

l) Share premium

m) Capital Redemption Reserve

n) Land and Buildings

o) Called up share capital not paid

p) Trade marks

q) Bills of exchange payable

r) Bank Loans

s) Revaluation reserve

t) Raw materials

u) Prepayments

v) Called up share capital

w) Other reserves

x) Pensions

Question 51

The General Trading Company Limited

The company is about to publish its annual accounts. What information must it show in relation to the income which it has earned during the last financial year?

a)

b)

c)

d)

What expenses must be shown against the firm's profits?

a)

b)

c)

d)

e)

f)

g)

h)

What information must be shown as to how the company has appropriated its profit?

a)

b)

c)

d)

Question 52

Plumbing Supplies Limited

The company has just prepared its annual accounts and the directors have decided to include a Value Added Statement. You have been given the following information and have been asked to prepare the statement for the 31 March Year Four.

	£
Taxation	40,000
Sales	324,000
Wages and employee benefits	75,000
Cost of goods sold	120,500
Interest Payments	14,000
Dividends	22,000
Depreciation of fixed assets	17,000
Retained profits	35,000

Question 53

Executive Stationery Supplies

Anita Saunders has been in business for one year selling office stationery. Last week she received her annual accounts but can't understand why some expenses have not been shown in the profit and loss account. You are currently working at the store, as part of your work experience, and she has asked you to answer the questions raised in her memo.

To: Trainee

From: Anita

Ref: Annual Acccounts

I need to know why the following information has not been treated as an expense in the firm's profit and loss account:

a) A van purchased for £12,000 has not been shown as an expense.

b) My office computer has been depreciated on its cost price, even though I enclosed a note saying that its market value is £200 more than the cost price.

c) The legal costs of purchasing the shop lease have not been shown in the profit and loss account, even though I sent a copy of the invoice to the accountants.

Question 54

Road Hauliers

This year the company bought a 40 ton truck for £40,000. The truck is expected to have a life of six years..

The firm expect the truck to have a residual value of 10% at the end of its working life. The directors depreciate their assets using the straight line method.

They would like you to:

a. Explain what is meant by the term *residual value*

b. Should the depreciation equal the current loss in market value?

c. Calculate the annual depreciation for the truck and show how it should be recorded in the firm's Balance Sheet.

Question 55

From the information given below, calculate the net book value of the following fixed assets:

	Asset	Cost	Depreciation to Date	Net Book Value
		£	£	£
a	Premises	165,000	22,000	?
b	Fixtures	50,000	10,000	?
c	Motor Van	8,700	2,700	?

Question 56

A company has just invested £50,000 in a new main frame computer system. The management believe that it will last five years, after which it will have no resale value. Calculate the depreciation for each year and show the asset's net book value and accumulated depreciation as it would appear in the firm's balance sheet at each year end, using the straight line method.

Question 57

A firm has just bought a lorry for £85,000. The firm depreciates all vehicles at 15% on the cost price of the asset. Calculate the depreciation and show the asset's net book value at each year end, using the Reducing Balance Method for the first five years.

Question 58

A firm bought a motor van for £12,000 three years ago and a lap top computer three years ago for £3,000. The firm depreciates the van at 20% a year and the computer at 25% a year on its cost price. Calculate the depreciation and the net book value for each year for both assets, using the Straight Line Method.

Question 59

A firm has bought a new electric saw at a cost of £10,000. It has been estimated that it will have a residual value of £2,000 and a working life of 60,000 hours. Calculate the depreciation charge per production hour.

Question 60

A ski centre has invested £100,000 in a new chair lift motor. The investment should have an operating life of 350,000 hours, after which the scrap value has been estimated to be 3% of its initial cost. Calculate the depreciation charge per hour.

Question 61

A new multi screen cinema has just invested £60,000 in new carpeting. The managment believe that it will have a life of ten years, after which time it will have no residual value. The cinema is open 360 days a year. Calculate the depreciation charge per day.

Question 62

A haulage company has just purchased a new truck for £85,000. It has been estimated that the engine will be good for 250 thousand miles. After that time its residual value has been estimated to be 7% of its cost price. Calculate the depreciation charge per mile.

Question 63

A manufacturing company has just bought a new machine for £20,000. The machine is capable of producing 50,000 units during its working life. Its residual value has been estimated at £1,500. Calculate the depreciation charge per unit produced.

Question 64

A company has just bought a new machine for £10,000. The machine is capable of producing 30,000 units during its working life, after which it will have no residual value. Calculate the depreciation charge per unit produced.

Question 65

A hotel has just invested £4,000 in a new deep freeze. The machine has been estimated to last five years, after which time it will have no residual value. Calculate the daily depreciation charge in using the machine (assume a 365 day year).

Question 66

European Hauliers

The company has just invested heavily in a new fleet of lorries and vans. You have been asked by your manager to calculate the annual depreciation (to the nearest whole number) for each vehicle, from the information shown in the table below, using the straight line method:

	Cost of Asset	Estimated Life Years	Estimated Residual Value	Depreciation Per Year
a	£34,000	6	£4,000	?
b	£70,000	10	£5,000	?
c	£69,240	8	£9,240	?
d	£12,000	3	NIL	?
e	£27,000	5	£2,000	?
f	£40,000	8	£6,000	?
g	£100,000	5	£15,000	?
h	£80,000	6	£24,000	?
i	£8,000	4	£1,500	?
j	£14,500	5	£2,750	?
k	£19,800	7	£1,500	?

Question 67

Plant Hire

Plant Hire purchase and rent out a range of equipment to the building industry. The firm has just invested in new capital equipment. You have been asked to calculate the annual depreciation and the assets' net book value after three years of ownership, using the reducing balance method.

	Cost £	Dep. Rate	Dep.Prov. Year One	Dep.Prov. Year Two	Dep.Prov. Year Three
a	30,000	12%			
b	47,000	10%			
c	12,000	20%			
d	28,000	15%			
e	60,000	25%			
f	25,000	14%			
g	10,000	5%			
h	40,000	14%			

The directors have just asked you to calculate the depreciation provisions for the same equipment, but using the straight line method.

	Cost £	Dep. Rate	Dep.Prov. Year One	Dep.Prov. Year Two	Dep.Prov. Year Three
a	30,000	12%			
b	47,000	10%			
c	12,000	20%			
d	28,000	15%			
e	60,000	25%			
f	25,000	14%			
g	10,000	5%			
h	40,000	14%			

Question 68

Zolan Limited

The company manufacture springs which are used in the motor industry. The firm's new factory can manufacture 20,000 springs a month. The firm's fixed costs are £40,000 a month. Recently the firm has been experiencing an erratic demand for its products. The firm's costs are shown below:

	50%	60%	70%	80%	90%	100%
Direct Materials (£6 per unit)						
Direct Labour (£4 per unit)						
Variable Overheads (£1.50 per unit)						
Fixed Costs						

1) Calculate the firm's total costs at the different levels of output.

2) If the selling price is £17, what is the contribution earned on each unit sold?

3) Calculate the profit which the firm will earn at each different level of output.

Question 69

Zoraq Limited

Zoraq manufacture components for the computer industry. One of their small industrial units has fixed costs of £20,000 a month. The firm's variable costs are £3 a unit and each one sells for £8. The management need to know how their costs and profits are affected by changes in output. The firm's output levels are shown below:

Output	Fixed Costs	Variable Cost	Sales	Profit
1,000				
2,000				
3,000				
4,000				
5,000				
6,000				
7,000				
8,000				
9,000				
10,000				
11,000				
12,000				
13,000				
14,000				
15,000				

Question 70

Markan Limited

The company manufacture a range of waterproof clothing. The firm's costs and sales are shown below for a pair of trousers which sell for £65.

Output Sales	Fixed Costs	Variable Costs	Profit
1,000	£30,000	£25 (per unit)	
2,000			
3,000			
4,000			
5,000			
6,000			
7,000			
8,000			
9,000			

The directors would like you to calculate the firm's costs and profits at different levels of activity.

Question 71

The Electric Motor Company

Electric Motors manufacture a range of motors which are used in consumer appliances. The company has just built a modern factory close to one of its other plants to manufacture engines for lawn mowers. The costs and output figures are shown below.

Fixed Costs Per Quarter	£250,00
Direct Materials	£5 0.00
Direct Labour	£ 28.00

The directors have asked you to calculate the costs and profit for the following levels of output:

Output Per Month	Total Fixed Cost £	Fixed Cost Per Unit £	Total Variable Cost £	Variable Cost Per Unit £
0				
500				
1,000				
3,000				
6,000				
10,000				
15,000				
30,000				
45,000				
50,000				
60,000				

Note

Round all Numbers to the nearest whole number.

Question 72

State which of the following costs should be classified as being direct or indirect.

Cost	Direct	Indirect
Materials		
Rent		
Direct Labour		
Supervisors' Wages		
Cleansing Materials		
Factory Insurance		
Rates		

Question 73

Calculate the variable cost per unit for Product X

	£	£	£	£
Prime Cost	54,000	43,200	129,600	91,800
Output	10,000	8,000	24,000	17,000
Cost Per Unit				

Question 74

Calculate the material cost per unit for Product Y

	£	£	£	£
Materials	6,750	13,500	33,750	19,125
Output	3,000	6,000	15,000	8,500
Cost Per Unit				

Question 75

Calculate the direct labour cost per unit of Product Z

	£	£	£	£
Labour Cost	44,100	31,500	75,600	94,500
Output	7,000	5,000	12,000	15,000

Question 76

If a firm has capacity to make 1,000 units a week and has fixed costs of £10,000, what will its fixed costs in total be if it operates at half capacity?

What will the final costs per unit be at the following levels of output?

Output	Fixed cost Per Unit
1	
100	
200	
300	
400	
500	
600	
700	
800	
900	
1000	

Question 77

Calculate the contribution from the following information

	£	£	£	£	£
Sales	30,000	25,000	17,900	65,000	83,700
Prime Cost	15,000	9,000	12,000	43,000	60,000
Contribution	?	?	?	?	?

Question 78

Calculate the contribution from the following information

	£	£	£	£	£
Sales	84,000	72,000	90,000	43,000	29,000
Materials	15,000	20,000	30,000	13,000	7,000
Direct Labour	20,000	15,000	40,000	10,000	12,000
Variable Overheads	4,000	6,000	12,000	9,000	3,000
Contribution	?	?	?	?	?

Question 79

Calculate the unit contribution from the following information

	£	£	£	£	£
Selling Price	20.90	30.00	45.50	60.30	90.00
Direct Materials	8.10	12.00	20,00	30.00	40.00
Direct Labour	4.00	7.00	9.00	12.00	20.00
Variable Overhead	1.23	2.50	3.67	4.25	2.90
Contribution	?	?	?	?	?

Question 80

If a firm has a productive capacity of 10,000 units per week and fixed costs of £10,000, what are its fixed costs per unit of output if the factory is operating at quarter capacity?

Question 81

You are working as a trainee in the cost accounting department and have been told that the variable cost per unit of output is £5.00. What will the unit variable cost be at the following levels of output? 300, 800, 1000?

Question 82

A travel company knows that the variable cost of travel is £10. What will be the total variable cost if it sells the following number of tickets? 50, 100, 150 and 200?

Question 83

From the following information calculate the contribution per unit:

	£	£	£	£
Selling Price	20.00	30.99	15.00	18.00
Direct Materials	7.20	15.40	8.90	7.00
Direct Labour	4.80	7.60	3.10	5.00
Contribution				

Question 84

Calculate the contribution to sales ratio from the following information:

	£	£	£	£
Selling Price	20	18	36	10
Contribution	10	6	10	2

Question 85

Calculate the break even point in units from the following information:

	£	£	£	£
Fixed Costs	45,000	30,000	27,000	48,000
Contribution	5	10	9	12
Units to B/Even				

Question 86

Calculate the break even point in sales from the following information:

	£	£	£	£
Sales	60,000	55,000	80,000	90,000
Prime Cost	20,000	15,000	40,000	29,000
Contribution				
Fixed Costs	15,000	25,000	30,000	35,000
Sales to B/Even				

Question 87

From the following information calculate the firm's margin of safety:

	£	£	£	£
Sales	45,600	100,000	89,000	73,000
Break Even	28,000	45,000	33,000	40,000
Margin of Safety				

Question 88

A firm can only market one new product next year. The selling price per unit and the prime cost per unit are shown below. Which product should the firm market?

Product	A	B	C	D
	£	£	£	£
Selling Price	18.00	24.00	30.00	40.00
Prime Cost	10.00	20.00	15.00	24.00

Question 89

A firm has calculated the contribution which it earns from the sale of each of its products. This week there are only enough workers to make one product. From the information given below, which one should it make?

Product	A	B	C	D
	£	£	£	£
Contribution	24.00	15.00	42.00	9.00
Labour Hours	4 hours	3 hours	6 hours	1 hour

Question 90

Monal Limited

Monal Limited manufacture electric cables. Its main factory is divided into three cost centres called EC1, EC2, EC3. The firm's costs and other information relating to the cost centres is shown below.

COSTS	
	£
Rent	10,000
Rates	4,500
Power	9,000
Supervision	16,000
Heating and Lighting	4,000
Depreciation of Plant	2,100

INFORMATION RE COST CENTRES EC1, EC2, and EC3			
	EC1	EC2	EC3
Area in square metres	500	450	250
Number of Employees	20	10	5
Value of Plant	£12,000	£6,000	£3,000
Machine Hours	2,000	1,500	1,000

You are currently working as a trainee management accountant and have been asked to prepare a statement showing how the firm's costs should be apportioned to each cost centre.

Question 91

Trees and Shrubs Limited

The company specalise in growing and planting a wide range of trees and garden shrubs. The firm has been divided into four cost centres G1, G2, G3 and G4. The costs and other information relating to the cost centres is shown below.

COSTS	
	£
Rent	30,000
Rates	8,000
Power	15,000
Supervision	24,000
Heating and Lighting	30,000
Depreciation of Plant	8,000
Insurance of Stocks	10,000

INFORMATION RE COST CENTRES G1, G2, and G3			
	G1	G2	G3
Area in square metres	500	450	250
Number of Employees	20	10	5
Value of Plant	£12,000	£6,000	£3,000
Machine Hours	2,000	1,500	1,000
Value of Stock	£10,000	£5,000	£2,000

You are currently working as a management trainee and have been asked to prepare a statement showing how the firm's costs should be apportioned to each cost centre.

Question 92

Adventure Parks Limited

The company operate a range of amusements on its twelve acre site. The Whirler is a very popular attraction and the costs of operating it are shown below.

	£
Insurance	400
Maintenance	500
Consumable Materials	100
Apportioned Costs	1,000
Operator's Wages	£5.00 per hour
Power	£1.00 per hour

The site is open for 360 days a year and for ten hours each day. The company estimate that the Whirler is idle about 10% of the time because of insufficient visitors.

You work for the company and have been asked to calculate the hourly cost of operating the machine.

Question 93

Harvest Pies

The company manufacture a range of oven ready meals at its factory in Oxford. The firm has just bought a new blending machine and the costs of operating it are shown below.

	£
Insurance	150
Maintenance	300
Consumable Materials	50
Apportioned Costs	2,400
Operator's Wages	£3.00 per hour
Power	£0.50 per hour

The factory operates a 261 day year and workers work a seven hour day. The company estimate that the blender will be idle for about 5% of the time.

You work for the company and have been asked to calculate the hourly cost of operating the machine.

Question 94

Hi Slope Skis

The firm is small and the owner does not understand cost accounting techniques, but has supplied you with the following information:

	October	November	December
Materials	£255,000	£289,000	£340,000
Labour	£180,000	£204,000	£240,000
Overheads	£ 93,500	£101,500	£113,500
Output	15,000	17,000	20,000
Selling Price	£50	£50	£50

Task

The owner would like to know:

(a) the unit variable cost of making a pair of skis for each month.

(b) the cost of manufacturing 25,000 skis.

(c) the break even point for the months of October, November and December, if the skis sell for £53 a pair.

Question 95

Bridge Hotel

You have just been appointed the manager of the Bridge Hotel, which has a large restaurant. The hotel is currently losing money and so the management have divided the business into cost centres. You have been appointed to return the business to profitability. At present the firm has no system of cost accounting, but you have been able to ascertain the following information.

	Jan	Feb	March	April	May
Number of meals served	20,000	25,000	33,000	40,000	45,000
	£	£	£	£	£
Cost of Food	94,800	118,500	156,420	189,600	213,300
Cost of Labour	25,800	32,250	42,570	51,600	58.050
Overheads	82,400	91,750	106,710	119,800	129,150

The average selling price of a meal in the restaurant is £12.50

You are required to calculate;

(a) the variable unit costs of the restaurant

(b) the fixed costs of the restaurant

(c) the contribution per meal sold

(d) the number of meals which must be sold for the restaurant to break even.

Question 96

Leaded Lights

The company specalise in making stained glass windows which are sold to numerous double glazing firms. During the last six months the firm has received unprecedented orders and the owner would like to use part of the profits to build an extension. Unfortunately he has been so busy that he has not been able to keep a tight control on costs, but has nevertheless been able to supply you with the following information.

	May	June	July	Aug	Sept	Oct
Units Made	500	620	700	840	900	940
	£	£	£	£	£	£
Glass	4,500	5,580	6,300	7,560	8,100	8,460
Direct Labour	2,315	2,871	3,241	3,889	4,167	4,352
Overheads	11,285	11,593	11,799	12,159	12,313	12,416

a) What are the firm's unit variable costs of production?

b) What are the fixed costs?

Question 97

Geoff's Garage

Geoffrey Roland has been self employed for ten years. He owns a small garage which services all makes of cars and is currently considering buying an additional hydraulic ramp to undertake routine oil and filter changes (as part of a while-you-wait service for customers).

A new ramp will cost £5,000 and will last five years. A good quality oil can be purchased at £5 for 5 litres and the average price of an oil filter is £3.50. A new employee will have to be recruited, which will cost £12,000 in wages, and other overheads will amount to £7,000. Customers will pay £14.50 per service and Geoffrey has approached his bank manager to ask for permission to increase the overdraft.

The bank manager has agreed to lend the money, once she knows the contribution earned from each service, and the number of filter changes required for the business to break even. George has asked your advice and would like you to:

a) explain to him what is meant by the term break even?

b) to calculate the firm's break-even point?

Question 98

Watch Straps

Watch Straps manufacture a range of metal watchstraps which are sold to retail outlets in the United Kingdom. For the first quarter of this year the costs and sales were as follows:

	January	February	March
Output	6,000	8,500	9,400
	£	£	£
Variable Cost	12,000	17,000	18,800
Fixed Costs	10,000	10,000	10,000
Sales	72,000	102,000	112,800

The directors would like to know:

(a) The marginal cost of making each watch strap

(b) The contribution earned from each sale

(c) The total contribution earned towards fixed costs from each month's trading

Question 99

Down at Heel

Mr and Mrs Jarvis have decided to invest part of their redundancy payments in a shoe repair shop close to a railway station. The shop rent is £25,000 a year, and the business must also pay insurance of £3,000 and leasing payments for equipment of £500 a month. The costs and selling prices of the repairs are shown below:

Shoe	Variable Cost	Repair Price
	£	£
Men's	2.50	4.00
Women's	1.45	2.75
Children's	0.95	1.50

The firm has budgeted to repair 100,000 pairs of shoes a year. 30,000 repairs will be men's shoes, 40,000 women's and the balance will be children's. Mr and Mrs Jarvis have asked you to calculate:

(a) What is the contribution earned from each category of shoe repaired?

(b) What is the firm's profit if its sales are the same as budgeted?

(c) Which repair will achieve the lowest break-even point for the firm?

Question 100

The Potter's Wheel

Last year Julie Young decided to set up a small business making and selling a range of clay flower pots. Recently the firm has been experiencing cash flow problems and her bank manager has advised her to concentrate on making her best selling lines. Julie knows that each month she sells 200 units of her brightly coloured patio pots but she is uncertain which one contributes the most to the firm's profits and cash flow. The costs, selling prices and time taken to manufacture the patio flower pot is shown below:

	Small	Medium	Large
	£	£	£
Selling Price	7.00	9.00	11.00
Clay	1.50	2.00	2.50
Paint	0.75	1.10	2.00
Variable Overheads	1.00	1.25	1.50
Manufacturing Time	2 hours	3 hours	4 hours

(a) What is the marginal cost of each patio flower pot?

(b) What is the contribution earned from each product sold?

(c) Which product should Julie concentrate on making?

Question 101

Tailored Suits

Tailored Suits manufacture a range of three business suits which are produced in grey, brown and blue wool. The relevant costs, sales and time to make each suit are shown below:

Product	Sales (units)	Selling Price	Marginal Cost	Time to Manufacture Garment
		£	£	
Grey	3,000	115	80	5 hours
Brown	1000	140	95	6 hours
Blue	5,000	99	64	7 hours

The directors would like to know:

(a) The contribution earned from each suit sold

(b) The total contribution earned from its sales

(c) Which suit the firm should concentrate on producing

72

Question 102

River Craft

River Craft manufacture three small boats which are sold mainly in the growing recreation markets. The boats are all made from wood and have proved very popular. The problem is that the company does not have enough skilled carpenters to manufacture all of the boats and the Production Director would like to know which boats should be made first. The costs and labour hours needed to build a boat are shown below;

	RC1	RC2	RC3
	£	£	£
Selling Price	250	400	375
Materials	85	149	120
Labour	65	180	90
Labour Hours	20	25	22

The company currently employ six carpenters who each work a forty-hour week.

73

Question 103

Smithdown Stores

Smithdown Stores is a medium sized department store. Last year the shop was divided into six different cost centres, for which sales and costs are shown below:

Department	Sales	Variable	Fixed
	£	£	£
Men's Wear	120,000	87,000	25,000
Women's Wear	180,000	110,000	40,000
Furniture	78,000	60,000	20,000
Hair Salon	40,000	12,000	10,000
Restaurant	70,000	35,000	15,000
Electrical Goods	95,000	70,000	25,000

The management of the store know that their business is currently losing money. They are anxious to increase their profits and are aware of rising competition in the retailing sector. As a result they have asked you to advice them whether or not they should consider closing the loss-making departments and letting out the top floor, which they believe could earn the firm £40,000 a year in rent.

Question 104

Metal Forge Masters

Metal Forge Masters have been invited to submit a tender to supply a new component for a series of cranes currrently being manufactured in Germany. The contract requires the firm to deliver one hundred components per month for three months and specifies that the unit cost should be in the following price range £600-£650. The costs of manufacturing each component are as follows:

	£
Direct Materials	200
Direct Labour	75
Variable Overheads	30

The firm has estimated that the fixed costs of production are £25,000 per month and the directors are anxious to secure the contract because the firm's order book is low. As a result, the directors have decided to submit a selling price of 5% above the minimum tender price.

You have been asked to calculate

(a) the marginal cost of making each component

(b) the contribution earned from each sale

(c) the number of components which must be made each month if the firm is to break even.

Question 105

Carpets and Curtains

Emma Reeves owns a small business which specialises in selling fabric and making curtains. She has just received an order from a builder who wants curtains made for a luxury detached house which is being built to customer specifications. Unfortunately she is very busy at the moment, but she has decided to accept the order even if it means subcontracting the work to a competitor. She has two identical jobs to finish for next week but she is unsure which job to keep in house. The costs for both jobs are shown below.

	Job A		Job B
	£		£
Selling Price		1,400	1,200
Direct Materials	600		460
Direct Labour	200		170
Direct Expenses	50		80
Fixed Overheads	400		340
Total Cost		1,250	1,050
Profit		150	150

As both jobs yield the same profit, Emma believes that it does not matter which job is subcontracted. Nevertheless she has decided to seek your advice as a financial consultant. Advise Emma.

Question 106

Southern Cross Hotel

Last year the Southern Cross Hotel chain opened a new hotel in Docklands. The hotel is currently losing money on some of its restaurants and the sales and costs are shown below:

	Docklands Restaurant	City Life Restaurant	Waterside Restaurant
	£	£	£
Sales	80,000	150,000	197,000
Food Costs	25,000	45,000	63,000
Labour	25,000	35,000	45,000
Overheads	40,000	40,000	40,000

The company has calculated that 30% of its overhead costs are variable. The owners would like to know:

(a) The profit currently earned from each restaurant?

(b) Whether or not they should close one restaurant?

Question 107

Central Theme Parks

The Central Theme Park Company has invested in three major attractions at their new site in Leicestershire. Unfortunately one of the attractions has been operating at a loss. The management are currently below their budgeted profit targets and are keen to eliminate any loss making facilities. They would like you to prepare a financial statement showing whether or not they should close the loss making attraction and have presented you with the following information:

Attraction	Shark Ride	The Swamp	The Tunnel
	£	£	£
Sales	130,000	90,000	225,000
Variable Costs	50,000	35,000	70,000
Direct Labour	35,000	15,000	40,000
Fixed Overheads	65,000	20,000	55,000

Question 108

Leather Crafts

Leather Crafts manufacure a range of leather handbags aimed at the top end of the ladies' fashion market. Recently the company has been experiencing increased competition from German and Italian manufacturers and the recession has led to the firm having to place its workers on short time. The factory is currently only operating at 50% capacity.

The company has just won a large order to make a range of handbags for a Spanish Fashion House, but the marketing director is worried about the tight profit margins as the selling price has been reduced by 40%. The relevant costs are shown below.

	£
Selling Price	120
Materials	40
Labour	25
Overheads	24,000

The firm has the capacity to make 850 handbags per month.

You have been asked to assess whether or not the firm should accept the order from the Spanish Fashion House.

Question 109

Leisure Cruises

Leisure Cruises manufacture three dinghies which they codename the Dh1, Dh2 and Dh3. The firm are currently facing fierce competition from abroad and the management are anxious to eliminate any loss-making products.

The budgeted sales and cost figures have just been prepared. They show product Dh1 and Dh2 making a profit, while Dh3 makes a loss. The budgeted figures are shown below.

Product	Dh1	Dh2	Dh3
	£	£	£
Sales	150,000	200,000	75,000
Direct Materials	47,000	60,000	35,000
Direct Labour	50,000	70,000	40,000
Overheads	20,000	30,000	10,000
Profit (Loss)	33,000	40,000	(10,000)

Note: Overheads 20% variable 80% fixed

Required

(a) Prepare a statement showing whether or not the firm should stop making product Dh3. (The statement should show the budgeted profit if the product is made and if it is abandoned.)

(b) Why is an understanding of the behaviour of costs important when considering future production levels?

80

Question 110

The South West Brewing Company

The firm is a small family-owned brewery. It sells its products under own label as well as brewing own-label brands for several of the large supermarket chains. The brewery is currently operating at 100% capacity but demand is seasonal. The directors have decided to adopt a flexible budgeting system so that they can ascertain costs at different levles of activity. .

Cost	£
Rent	70,000
Rates	15,000
Prime costs	90,000
Insurance	10,000
Indirect Labour	20,000
Advertising	5,000

You work for the company and have been asked to prepare a flexible budget for the firm showing its costs at the following levels of activity: 70, 80, 90, 100.

Question 111

The Wooden Fencing Company

A company manufactures a range of ready assembled wooden fences. It is currently operating at 100% capacity, but the managment know that demand for its products are very dependent upon the weather. As a result they have decided to prepare a flexible budget for different levels of possible activity. The costs below show the firm's annual operating costs at 100% activity, but for short periods the firm can operate at 110% capacity by working overtime.

Cost	£
Rent	100,000
Rates	20,000
Direct Materials	600,000
Direct Labour	450,000
Power	120,000
Factory Insurance	20,000
Indirect Labour	30,000

You work for the company and have been asked to prepare a flexible budget showing costs at the following levels of activity 80, 90, 100, and 110%.

Question 112

R and H Metal Manufacturers

The company produce metal springs used in the car industry and face fierce competition from both Far Eastern and European manufacturers. The firm's management believe that, if fixed costs could be reduced by 3%, sales could be increased by 9%. During the coming year raw materials are expected to rise by 5% and wages by 7%. Variable Overhead costs are expected to increase by 6%.

Last year's profit and loss account is shown below.

R and H Metal Manufacturing Profit and Loss Account for the year ending 4 April Year 7		
	£	£
Sales		870,000
Less Costs		
Raw Materials	155,000	
Wages	130,000	
Variable Overheads	37,000	
Fixed Overheads	52,000	374,000
Profit		496,000

Based on the company's forecasts, the directors would like you to prepare the budgeted profit and loss account for the company.

Question 113

The Malaysian Restaurant

The Malaysian Restaurant specialises in selling Malaysian food in North London. The owner faces fierce competition from other restaurants in the area and believes that, if restaurant prices could be reduced by 5%, sales could be increased by 12%.

During the coming year food costs are expected to rise by 4% and wages by 6.1%. The restaurant also faces a £2,000 increase in its rent. Last year's profit and loss account is shown below.

The Malaysian Restaurant's Profit and Loss Account for the year ending 31 January Year 5.		
	£	£
Sales		100,000
Less Costs		
Food Costs	30,000	
Wages	25,000	
Variable Overheads	7,000	
Fixed Overheads	20,000	82,000
Profit		18,000

You are required to:

(a) Prepare a forecast budgeted profit and loss account.

(b) Write a report outlining how a system of budgetary control can help a business to control its costs.

84

Question 114

Material Usage Variances

Calculate the following variances

(a) A bakery has set a standard cost of 30p per kg of flour and a standard usage per week of 1,000 kg. The bakery manager has used 1,200 kg at 33p per kg. Calculate the direct usage variance.

(b) A property company has set a standard cost of 40p a brick and a standard usage of 3,000 bricks per week. The site manager has used 2,700 bricks. Calculate the direct usage variance.

(c) A shipping company has set a standard cost of 46p a litre of gas oil and a standard usage per week of 8,000 litres. The master has used 9,000 litres. Calculate the direct usage variance.

(d) A woollen company has set a standard cost of 80p per ounce of wool and a standard usage of 5,000 ounces per month. The mill manager has used 5,500 ounces. Calculate the direct usage variance.

(e) A fast food restaurant has set a standard cost of 32p per pint of milk and a standard usage of 2,000 pints per week. The restaurant manager has used 1,700 pints. Calculate the direct usage variance.

(f) A tailor has set a standard cost of £80 for materials and a usage of 20 lengths of cloth per month. The firm has actually used 18 lengths. Calculate the direct usage variance.

Question 115

Direct Labour Variances

Calculate the following variances

(a) A garage has set a standard cost for servicing a car of 3 hours at £17 an hour. The work was completed in 2 hours at a cost of £15 an hour. Calculate the direct labour variance.

(b) A dry cleaners has set a standard time of cleaning a suit of one hour at £3 an hour. The work was completed in one and a half hours at a cost of £2 an hour. Calculate the direct labour variance.

(c) A carpet factory has set a standard time of making a roll of carpet at five hours at £10 an hour. The work was completed in 11 hours at £9 an hour. Calculate the direct labour variance.

(d) A farmer has set a standard time of ploughing a hectare at 2 hours at £4 an hour. The work was completed in two hours. Calculate the direct labour variance.

(e) A delivery firm has set a standard time of driving to a customer of 1 hour at a cost of £8 per hour. The time taken was 2 hours at a cost of £8 per hour. Calculate the direct labour variance.

(f) A hotel has set a standard time of cleaning a conference suite of 2 hours at a cost of £7 per hour. The time taken was one and a half hours. Calculate the direct labour variance.

Question 116

Material Price Variances

Calculate the following Variances

(a) A bakery has set a standard cost of 30p per kg of flour and a standard usage per week of 1,000 kg. The bakery manager has ordered 1,200 kg at 33p per Kg. Calculate the direct material price variance.

(b) A property company has set a standard cost of 40p a brick and a standard usage of 3,000 bricks per week. he site manager has ordered 2,700 bricks at a cost of 38p a brick. Calculate the direct material price variance.

(c) A shipping company has set a standard cost of 46p a litre of gas oil and a standard usage per week of 8,000 litres. The master has ordered 9,000 litres at 47p a litre. Calculate the direct material price variance.

(d) A woollen company has set a standard cost of 80p per ounce of wool and a standard usage of 5,000 ounces per month. The mill manager has ordered 5,500 ounces at a cost of 83p an ounce. Calculate the direct material price variance.

(e) A fast food restaurant has set a standard cost of 32p per pint of milk and a standard usage of 2,000 pits per week. The restaurant manager has used 1,700 pints at a cost of 31p a pint. Calculate the direct material price variance.

(f) A tailor has set a standard cost of £80 for materials and a usage of 20 lengths of cloth per month. The firm has actually paid £75 per length of cloth and used 18 lengths. Calculate the direct material price variance.

Question 117

Executive Traveller

The company manufacture a range of expensive leather cases and holdalls. The firm has experienced record growth but the directors are anxious to monitor costs and have set up a standard costing system. The costs for their best selling range are shown below:

	Budgeted Output	Standard Cost	Actual Cost
		£	£
Sales	25,000	45	950,000
Materials		20	450,000
Labour		10	300,000
Variable Overheads		7	175,000
Fixed Overheads		4	112,500

You work for the firm as a trainee accountant and have been asked to calculate the costing trading and profit and loss account and to compare the budgeted with the actual profit.

Question 118

The Kitchen Mouldings Company

The company manufactures a range of kitchen accessories for both the consumer and the industrial market. A standard costing system is in operation and the half yearly output level, together with the standard costs for one product, is shown below:

	Budgeted Output	Standard Cost	Actual Cost
		£	£
Sales	15,000	10	130,000
Materials		3	48,500
Labour		2	27,000
Factory Variable Overheads		1	15,000
Factory Overheads Fixed		1	14,000

The directors have asked you to prepare the firm's costing trading and profit and loss account and to compare the budgeted with the actual profit.

Question 119

Irons and Woods

For nearly one hundred years the company has made golf clubs. The clubs are highly regarded by both professionals and amateurs. They operate a standard costing system and has set its quarterly output level, together with the standard costs for their best selling range of clubs. The costs are shown below:

	Budgeted Output	Standard Cost	Actual Cost
		£	£
Sales	30,000	45	27,000
Materials		24	204,000
Labour		12	123,000
Factory Overheads		6	48,000

The directors have asked you to prepare the firm's trading and profit and loss account in marginal costing format and to compare the budgeted with the actual profit.

Question 120

The Welsh Honey Farm

The management of the farm are preparing their six monthly cash forecast. They have decided to accept a large export order and have arranged an overdraft facility of £40,000. The owners are anxious not to exceed the firm's overdraft limit and have asked you to prepare a six months' cash forecast from the following information.

	Jan £	Feb £	Mar £	Apr £	May £	June £
Sales	65,000	73,000	120,000	140,000	110,000	130,000
Variable costs	33,000	40,000	70,000	85,000	65,000	80,000
Fixed Costs	15,000	15,000	20,000	20,000	20,000	20,000
Taxation		8,000			22,000	
Dividends			35,000			

Note:

On the 1 January the firm has a credit balance at the bank of £15,000.

Question 121

The Woollen Rug Company

The management at the company are preparing their six monthly cash forecast. The firm is already in overdraft and must not exceed a £150,000 overdraft facility. The directors have asked you to prepare the firm's cash budget and advise them should they be in any danger of exceeding their overdraft limit.

	Jan	Feb	Mar	Apr	May	June
Sales (units at £40 per unit)	930	975	1,200	980	1020	1300
Raw Materials	16,740	17,550	21,600	17,640	15,120	14,166
Labour Costs	7,440	7,800	9,600	7,840	6,720	6,296
Variable Overheads	2,790	2,925	3,600	2,940	2,520	2,361
Fixed Overheads	9,000	9,000	9,000	9,000	9,000	9,000
New Machinery		15,000		8,000		
Leasing Payments	800	800	800	800	800	800
Taxation			33,000			

Note:

On the 1 January the firm's overdraft was £47,859.

Question 122

Leather Boots Ltd

The company manufacture a range of boots for the industrial and leisure market. The budgeted production and sales are shown below. You work in the firm's Finance Department and have been asked to prepare the firm's cash budget for the following six months.

Budgeted Production and Sales Figures

PRODUCTION (pairs)			
Dec	Jan	Feb	March
4,200	3,400	2,100	2,400
April	May	June	
1,750	1,500	1,400	
SALES (pairs)			
Dec	Jan	Feb	March
3,500	3,000	1,800	2,000
April	May	June	
1,900	1,300	1,100	

The firm has the additional costs

1) Raw materials used in production are £12 a unit.

2) Direct labour costs are £6 per unit.

3) All prime costs are payable in the month of production.

93

4) The firm pays leasing charges of £2,000 a month.

5) Variable overheads are £8,000 a month, one quarter of which is payable in the month of production. The balance is payable the following month.

6) Factory rent is £8,000 a month.

7) All goods are sold on one month's credit but past experience shows that 25% of the firm's debtors pay in the month in which the goods are sold. The remainder pay the following month.

8) The leather boots are sold for £39.

9) The company currently has a £60,000 cash balance.

Question 123

The Griffin Paint Company

At the main factory on the outskirts of Cardiff the firm manufactures specialist paints used by the aerospace industry. The budgeted costs and selling price for the coming six months are shown below. You have been asked to prepare the firm's cash budget for the next six months' trading.

Griffin Paint — Costs per Litre	
	£
Direct Materials	20
Direct Labour	5
Variable Overheads	2
Selling Price	47

Additional Information

1) The firm has fixed costs of £15,000 per month.

2) All direct labour costs are paid in the month in which they are incurred.

3) The firm receives two months' credit for raw materials purhased.

4) The firm pays 25% of its variable overhead costs in the month in which they are incurred and the balance the following month.

5) The firm has £800 leasing payments per month.

6) The firm must repay a £10,000 loan repayment in May.

7) The firm sells 20% of its output for cash with the balance being received one month after sale.

8) The paint is sold at £25 per litre.

9) On the 1 January the company had an overdraft 0f £80,000.

Budgeted Production and Sales Figures			
PRODUCTION			
<u>Litres</u>			
Nov	**Dec**	**Jan**	**Feb**
1,000	1,200	1,400	1,400
March	**April**	**May**	**June**
1,100	1,250	900	850
SALES			
<u>Litres</u>			
Nov	**Dec**	**Jan**	**Feb**
900	1,000	1,200	1,500
March	**April**	**May**	**June**
800	950	700	800

Question 124

In a Cash Flow Statement indicate whether the following would be shown as a source or an application of funds.

		Source	Application
a	Decrease in debtors		
b	Increase in stock		
c	Reduction in bank overdraft		
d	Dividend Payments		
e	Corporation tax		
f	Increase in retained profits		
g	Increase in creditors		
h	Sale of fixtures and fittings		
i	Profit on the sale of fixed assets		
j	Redemption of debentures		
k	Purchase of new premises		
l	Issue of shares at a premium		
m	Depreciation of fixed assets		
n	Redemption of debentures at a premium		
o	Writing off goodwill		
p	Issue of new shares		

Question 125

Which of the following would be a source or an application of funds in a Cash Flow Statement?

		Source	Application
a	Purchase of fixed assets		
b	Issue of secured loan stock		
c	Increase in debtors		
d	Decrease in stock		
e	Share Premium		
f	Decrease in bank overdraft		
g	Increase in creditors		
h	Increase in bank term loan		
i	Depreciation of Plant and Equipment		
j	Purchase of motor vehicles		
k	Increase in W.I.P.		
l	Decrease in cash		

Question 126

Which of the following would be a source or an application of funds?

		Source	Application
a	Increase in bank overdraft		
b	Profit		
c	Depreciation of fixed assets		
d	Issue of shares		
e	Repayment of a loan		
f	Decrease in creditors		
g	Increase in stock		
h	Premium payable on redemption of debentures		
i	Increase in cash		
j	Sale of fixed assets		
k	Increase in creditors		
l	Payment of Dividends		
m	Rights Issue		
n	Investment Income		

Question 127

The Rose Garden Nursery

Balance Sheet as at 31 December Year 7				
	Year 6		Year 7	
	£	£	£	£
Fixed Assets				
Premises		30,000		30,000
Machinery		10,000		17,000
Motor Vehicles		-		5,000
		40,000		52,000
Current Assets				
Stock	15,000		35,000	
Debtors	5,000		20,000	
Bank & Cash Balance	7,000		17,000	
		27,000		72,000
Less Current Liabilities				
Creditors		6,000		21,000
Bank Loan		-		10,000
Net Assets		61,000		93,000
Financed By				
Ordinary Share Capital		60,000		60,000
Profit & Loss Account		1,000		33,000
		61,000		93,000

The owners would like to know why they seem to be constantly short of cash, even though the business is profitable. They have asked you to prepare an accounting statement which shows the cash flow of funds during the last financial year.

Question 128

The Patisserie

Balance Sheet as at 31 December Year 4

	Year 3 £	Year 4 £
Fixed Assets		
Premises	60000	80000
Motor Vehicles	10000	17000
	70000	97000
Current Assets		
Stock	15000	27000
Debtors	11000	21000
Bank & Cash Balances	8000	13000
	34000	61000
Less Current Liabilities		
Creditors	9000	10000
Net Assets	95000	148000
Financed By		
Ordinary Share Capital	95000	105000
Profit & Loss Account	-	28000
Long Term Loans	-	15,000
	95000	148000

The following is required:

(a) Prepare a Cash Flow Statement .

(b) Write a report to the Board of Directors explaining the statement.

Question 129

The Whole Wheat Bakery

The company was started three years ago by Mr and Mrs Prescott who believed that there was a market for bread baked with organically-grown flour. The business has been successful and supplies both retail and catering companies.

For the last three months the firm has been in overdraft and each month the overdraft figure increases. Mr and Mrs Prescott cannot understand how this can be the case. The firm is selling 20% more than the same quarter last year and credit sales to companies are up 14%. Unfortunately the firm's cash shortage has led to problems in paying suppliers and many are now demanding cash with orders.

The owners have received a letter from their bank manager warning them that the firm must not exceed its overdraft position and inviting Mr and Mrs Prescott to visit the manager to discuss the current working capital problems. Mr And Mrs Prescott have sought your advice and have asked you the following questions:

(a) What is working capital?

(b) How can a profitable firm be short of cash?

(c) What action should the firm take to improve its cash flow?

Question 130

Acquarians Ltd.

The directors of Acquarians Limited know that their manufacturing processes are long. Recently the company has been experiencing cash flow problems and have given you extracts from their last set of annual accounts. They would like you to calculate their cash operating cycle and write them a brief report outlining the changes which have taken place in the last two years.

Extract of Profit and Loss Account and Balance Sheet as at

	Last Year	This Year
	£	£
Sales	260,000	480,000
Cost of Goods Sold	74,000	179,000
Purchases of raw materials	58,000	93,340
Debtors	14,300	42,000
Creditors	8,240	37,500
Raw Material Stock	22,000	79,000
Work in Progress	14,600	47,450
Finished Goods Stock	22,000	48,000
Cost of goods made	33,000	72,500
Raw materials used	65,000	165,000

You should assume that all sales and purchases are on credit.

Question 131

Barton Lodge Crafts

During the past year Barton Lodge Crafts Ltd have experienced cash flow problems. They have provided you with the following financial information:

Extract of Profit and Loss Account and Balance Sheet as at		
	Last Year £	This Year £
Sales	500,000	650,000
Purchase of raw materials	175,000	260,000
Raw Materials used in Production	190,000	240,000
Cost of goods manufactured	390,000	525,000
Cost of goods sold	370,000	490,000
Debtors	80,000	120,000
Creditors	6,000	9,000
Stocks - Raw Materials	30,000	45,000
Work in Progress	45,000	60,000
Finished goods	30,000	75,000
All purchases and sales made on credit.		

Task

(a) From the above data, calculate the business' cash generating cycle.

Question 132

What do the following Ratios seek to measure?

	Ratio	Calculation	Assessment
a	Acid Test		
b	Primary Ratio		
c	Gearing Ratio		
d	Interest Cover		
e	Current Ratio		
f	Dividend Yield		
g	Earnings Per Share		
h	Stock Turnover		
i	Debtors Collection Period		
j	Price to Earnings		

Question 133

The Diverse Engineering Group

"Any shareholder who bought shares in the company during the last eighteen months has seen the value of their investment drastically reduced. Yesterday the shares dropped another 10p to an all time low of £1.27 and most financial analysts are convinced that the company is not yet out of the wood.

The group's problems can be traced back to the time when it embarked upon a huge acquisition programme in Germany and the United States. Corporate borrowings rose dramatically as a whole range of engineering firms were purchased. For a while profits rose but a series of problems in North America, coupled with currency fluctuations, has dramatically reduced corporate profits.

Today corporate debts stand at 70% of total assets and, although the company has not yet approached its bankers to reschedule its debts, many people in the City wonder how long the group can remain so highly geared.

Fortunately the company is still profitable and stringent cash control measures have helped to secure institutional support at least for the short term. Still the shares remain only for the very brave but, if the Chair Linda Johnson is right, financial rewards could flow once the North American market moves out of recession."

Robert Walters
Financial Correspondent

(a) What are the dangers of pursuing an acquisition policy with debt capital?

(b) Why might the firm need to restructure its debts in the future?

(c) Why might Linda Johnson be right in thinking that the shares could perform well in the future?

Question 134

Transic plc

The Transic Group have just placed an advertisement in the national papers to advertise the group's results.

Extract from Chair's statement

" Profits and sales continue to rise in a year when trading conditions have been badly affected by the recession"

Summary of the Group's Results		
	Last Year	This Year
	£	£
Turnover	3,500,000	4,250,000
Trading Profit	800,000	910,000
Net Interest	40,000	65,000
Profit on ordinary activities before taxation	760,000	845,000
Taxation	250,000	300,000
Profit for the financial year attributable to shareholders	510,000	545,000
Dividends	80,000	90,000
Profit Retained	470,000	455,000
Earnings Per Share	17p	18.25p

The company have decided to send a brief explanation to all shareholders before the published accounts are despatched. You have been asked to explain the information shown in the above advertisement.

Question 135

The Takeover Battle

The Traveller's Friend and Overseas Visitor are two companies which have made a niche market in providing cut price holidays to travellers wishing to go on holiday at short notice. The directors of Overseas Visitor have just launched a takeover bid for the other company and are appealing to shareholders to accept the offer, arguing that they can make greater returns for the shareholders.

The directors of Overseas Travel have just issued the following advertisement.

Advertisement

It's not the capital base which is important but the returns made from it. Last year both companies had similar turnover with an identical capital base and yet we outperformed Traveller's Friend. Just look at the figures:

	Traveller's Friend	Overseas Visitor
	£	£
Called up Share Capital	250,000	150,000
Debentures	50,000	100,000
Unsecured Loan Stock	50,000	50,000
Capital Employed	300,000	300,000
Return on Capital Employed	14%	25%
Earnings per Share	15p	27p
Gross Dividend	6p	11p
Average Share Price	£1.34	£2.45

Looking at the capital base of the two companies:

(a) Which company is the more highly geared?

(b) Which is the riskier company to invest in?

(c) How can Overseas Visitor afford to pay higher dividends?

(d) If you were considering purchasing 1,000 shares in either company, which one would you choose?

Question 136

Harlequin Tours

The company directors would like to acquire new premises in Holland and set up a holiday company in Belgium. The holiday market is currently expanding rapidly and the firm is anxious to take advantage of the growth in European Travel. The directors have asked you as a corporate finance consultant how they should raise the money. They have supplied you with the following information.

Extract of Current Balance Sheet as at Year 10	
Capital	£
500,000 £1 shares issued and fully paid	500,000
Share Premium	100,000
12% Debenture 2010-2012	300,000
Capital Employed	900,000

The directors are considering raising the company's borrowing by issuing the following loan stocks:

£100,000 12% Unsecured Loan Stock 1999

£200,000 10% debenture Stock — 2020

Increasing the company's overdraft facility from £60,000 to £100,000.

(a) How would the proposed new capital affect the company's capital base?

(b) What are the dangers in raising so much debt finance?

(c) Why may the company be reluctant to issue more equity finance?

Question 137

The Wine Grotto

The Wine Grotto is a chain of off licences in the North East of England. The directors have just received extracts from the audited accounts and they are shown below:

Profit and Loss Account for the year ending year 5		
	£'000	£'000
Sales		460
Cost of goods sold		220
Gross Profit		240
Wages	50	
Overheads	30	
		80
Net Profit		160
Balance Sheet as at end of year 5		
Fixed Assets		400
Current Assets		
Stock	80	
Debtors	120	
Bank	400	
	600	
Less Current Liabiliies		
Creditors	300	300
Net Assets		700
Financed By		
Share Capital		600
Reserves		100
Shareholders' Funds		700

The directors have asked you to calculate the firm's

a) Current ratio

b) Acid Test ratio

c) Stock Turnover

d) Debtors' Turnover

e) Return on Capital Employed

Question 138

Calculate the pay back times for the following investments.

	Project TYA	Project TYB	Project TYC
Investment	£36,000	£69,000	£108,000
Life of Investment	3 Years	4 Years	4 Years
Year One Cash Inflow	£12,000	£24,000	£23,000
Year Two Cash Inflow	£24,000	£45,000	£42,000
Year Three Cash Inflow	£17,000	£37,000	£43,000
Year Four Cash Inflow	£ NIL	£29,000	£46,000

Pay Back Time   ?   ?   ?

Question 139

Calculate the pay back times for the following investments and write a memo to the Finance Director outlining which project represents the best investment.

	Project XZ1	Project XZ2	Project XZ3
Investment	£100,000	£235,000	£195,000
Life of Investment	4 Years	5 Years	6 Years
Year One Cash Inflow	£34,000	£52,000	£35,000
Year Two Cash Inflow	£39,000	£64,000	£52,000
Year Three Cash Inflow	£46,000	£77,000	£68,000
Year Four Cash Inflow	£55,000	£66,000	£96,000
Year Five Cash Inflow	£ NIL	£53,000	£87,000
Year Six Cash Inflow	£ NIL	£ NIL	£74,000

Pay Back Time   ?   ?   ?

Question 140

The committee at the Yacht Club are considering investing £30,000 in new facilities. They have estimated that the new investment will yield the following net cash inflows for the club:

Net Cash Inflows	£
Year One	8,100
Year Two	12,400
Year Three	14,500
Year Four	17,300
Year Five	15,200

You have been asked by the committee to write a memo outlining the accounting rate of return which the new investment should yield.

Question 141

A farmer is considering investing £80,000 in a new tractor and trailor. The annual estimated returns are shown below:

Net Cash Inflows	£
Year One	30,000
Year Two	45,600
Year Three	55,000
Year Four	63,000
Year Five	77,900

Calculate the accounting rate of return from the proposed new investment.

Question 142

Calculate the net present value of the following cash inflows to be received in the future, assuming the firm requires a 16% return on capital.

Year Cash	Inflow	Net Present Value
	£	£
1	33,540	
2	47,840	
3	66,300	
4	92,479	
5	102,580	
6	126,389	
7	167.394	

Question 143

Calculate the return an investment would receive after ten years on a capital sum of £10,000 at the following rates of compound interest:

Capital	5%	7%	10%	12%	15%
£ 10000					

Question 144

Calculate the future values of the following sums for the next ten years at the different rates of interest below:

£17,000	£20,000	£33,500	£45,700	£90,000	£66,000
8%	6%	10%	12%	4%	16%

Question 145

Year Cash	Cash Inflow	Net Present Value
	£	£
1	5,000	
2	14,300	
3	18,900	
4	26,700	
5	34,700	
6	44,590	
7	63,820	

Calculate the net present value of the following cash inflows to be received in the future, assuming the firm requires a 12% return on capital:

Question 146

Steel Stockholders Limited

During the last five years the company has seen an increased demand for high quality sheet steel and so it has decided to invest in new warehousing facilities. The new investment will cost £250,000 with additional cash outflows during the first three years. You work as a trainee manager in the Finance Department and have been asked to calculate the firm's cash flow table from the information given below.

Year	Investment £	Cash Inflow £	Cash Outflow £	Net Cash Flow £
0	(250,000)	-		
1	65,000	33.000		
2	79,000	22,000		
3	94,000	11,500		
4	125,000			
5	146,000			
6	157,000			

Question 147

Wood Supplies

The directors at Wood Supplies are considering building an extension which will enable them to hold larger stocks. The firm is currently short of working capital and has asked you to calculate a cash flow table from the following information.

Year	Investment	Cash Inflow	Cash Outflow	Net Cash Flow
	£	£	£	£
0	(180,000)	-	-	
1		25,000	7.000	
2		49,000	8,000	
3		66,000	15,000	
4		75,000	15,000	
5		83,000	10,000	
6		85,000	-	
7		90,000	-	

Question 148

The Village Lawn Tennis Club

The club's old hard courts are coming to the end of their working life. The club's managment committee have decided to invest in new hard courts and to convert two of the grass courts to hard ones. During the day the courts will be let out to a local school and this will generate additional income. The conversion of the grass courts will also save money and it is hoped that the new facilities will increase membership by 20% The costs, cash inflows and savings are shown below:

Year	Investment	Cash	Inflows Savings
	£	£	£
0	14,000	—	—
1	—	9,000	100
2	7,500	12,000	250
3	8,000	17,000	300
4	8,500	20,000	450
5	—	22,000	500
6	—	25,000	—

The club's committee have divided to finance the new improvements by selling some stocks and securities. These have averaged an 8% return over the last ten years and they would like the new investment to earn a similar return.

1 Calculate whether or not the proposed investment can earn an 8% return.

Question 149

Mountain Tours

Mountain Tours specalise in arranging hiking and climbing holidays in the Scottish mountains. They are considering investing £120,000 in a new chalet complex. They have built up a cash reserve of £40,000 but need to borrow the balance from their bank. Interest rates are currently 14% The estimated sales income from the chalets are:

	£
Year One	35,000
Year Two	57,000
Year Three	64,000
Year Four	70,000
Year Five	89,000

The directors would like to know if they should proceed with their investment plans and have asked you to calculate;

(a) the pay back time

(b) the accounting rate of return

(c) the net present value

Question 150

Travel Tours

Travel Tours are considering investing in a new coach. The cost of the coach is £65,000.

The firm has estimated that its future fares income will be as follows:

	£
Year One	26,000
Year Two	33,000
Year Three	36,000
Year Four	45,000
Year Five	48,000

The coach is being bought on hire purchase and the cost of the finance is 18%. The directors are worried about investing at a time when interest rates are so high and they have asked you to appraise their investment plans.

(a) What is the pay back time from the investment?

(b) What is the accounting rate of return?

(c) What is the investments net present value?

Suggested Answers

Answer 1 - Tube Masters

Finance Director:-	Financial Objectives, Planning, Raising Capital.
Financial Accountant:-	Stewardship, Profit and Loss Accounts Balance Sheets, Recording Financial Transactions.
Management Accountant:-	Costing, Budgeting, Analysis of Cost Variances.
Corporate Treasurer:-	Working Capital Control, Credit Policy Raising Long and Short Term Finance

Answer 2

Cash Book

DEBIT ENTRIES		CREDIT ENTRIES	
	£		£
Opening Balance	100	Stamps	20
Cash Sales	10	Rent 1	5
Cash Sales	30	Wages	20
Cash Sales	25	Petrol 1	2
		Stationery	5
		Bank	15
		Balance	78
	165		165

Answer 3

Credit balance £100

Answer 4

(a) Debit Bank, Credit Cash;   (b) Debit Stationery, Credit Bank;
(c) Debit Purchases, Credit Cash; (d) Debit Cash, Credit Sales;
(e) Debit Motor Van, Credit Bank; (f) Debit Purchases,Credit Bank
(g) Debit Petrol, Credit Cash,   (h)Debit Drawings, Credit Cash
(i) Debit Khan, Credit Sales,   (j) Debit Insurance, Credit Bank
(k) Debit Rent, Credit Bank.

Answer 5

(a) Debit Cash £1,000, Credit Capital £1,000
(b) Debit Bank £500, Credit Cash £500
(c) Debit Purchases £300, Credit Bank £300
(d) Debit Cash £200, Credit Sales £200
(e) Debit Office Equipment £600, Credit Bank £600
(f) Debit Bank £100, Credit Sales £100
(g) Debit Office Stationery £50, Credit Cash £50
(h) Debit Cash £500, Credit Capital £500
(i) Debit Cash £30, Credit Bank £30
(j) Debit Cleaning £5, Credit Cash £5.

Answer 6

Day	Ledgers	Debit £	Credit £
One	Cash Book	80	
	Purchases	40	
	Cash Book		40
	Cash Book	60	
	Sales		60
	Bank	10	
	Cash		10
Two	Purchases	30	
	Cash		30
	Milk	12.60	
	Cash		12.60
	Cleaning	4.30	
	Cash		4.30
	Cash	40	
	Sales		40
Three	Purchases	50	
	Cash		50
	Cash	90	
	Sales		90
	Heating	27.30	
	Cash		27.30
Four	Purchases	45	
	Cash		45
	Cash	70	
	Sales		70
	Laundry	15	
	Cash		15
	Bank	12	
	Cash		12
Five	Purchases	30	
	Cash		30
	Cash	45	
	Sales		45
	Wages	60	
	Cash		60
	Bank	20	
	Cash		20

Answer 7

	Ledgers	Account	Dr/Cr
b)	Bank	Real	Debit
	Cash	Real	Credit
c)	Purchases	Real	Debit
	GH Ltd	Personal	Credit
d)	Wages	Real	Debit
	Bank	Real	Credit
e)	Premises	Real	Debit
	Bank	Real	Credit
f)	Cash	Real	Debit
	Sales	Personal	Credit
g)	Telephone	Real	Debit
	Cash	Real	Credit
h)	Computer	Real	Debit
	KL Supplies	Personal	Credit
i)	H Ltd	Real	Debit
	Sales	Personal	Credit
j)	Purchases	Real	Debit
	Cash	Real	Credit
k)	Cash	Real	Debit
	Bank	Real	Credit
l)	Insurance	Real	Debit
	Bank	Real	Credit
m)	Cash	Real	Debit
	Asset Disposal	Real	Credit

Note: To distinguish between real and personal. Real Accounts are assets and Expense Accounts found in the nominal ledger. Personal Accounts are individual accounts to be found in the purchase or sales ledger.

Answer 8

(a) Credit,   (b) Credit,   (c) Debit,   (d) Debit,   (e) Credit
(f) Credit,   (g) Debit,   (h) Debit,   (i) Debit,   (j) Debit
(k) Debit,   (l) Debit,   (m) Debit,   (n) Debit,   (o) Debit,
(p) Debit,   (q) Debit,   (r) Debit,   (s) Credit,   (t) Debit
(u) Credit,   (v) Debit   (w) Debit   (x) Debit,   (y) Debit,
(z) Credit

Answer 9 - The Tool Box

Trial Balance 5 April Year One

	Dr.	Cr.
	£	£
Sales		45,890
Commission Received		1,540
Freehold Premises	73,000	
Purchases	22,583	
Motor Van	800	
Heat and Light	300	
Wages	700	
Carriage Inwards	200	
Office Cleaning	340	
Rent and Rates	1,350	
Discount Received		400
Discount Allowed	230	
Fixtures and Fittings	2,560	
Debtors	8,300	
Creditors	22,000	
Bank Loan	1,500	
Motor Expenses	400	
Returns Inwards	100	
Capital		86,533
	134,363	134,363

Answer 10

(a) Asset   (b) Liability (c) Liability (d) Asset   (e) Liability
(f) Asset   (g) Asset   (h) Liability (i) Asset   (j) Liability
(k) Asset   (l) Asset   (m) Liability (n) Asset   (o) Liability
(p) Liability (q) Asset   (r) Asset   (s) Liability (t) Liability

Answer 11

(a) Asset   (b) Liability (c) Asset   (d) Liability (e) Asset
(f) Liability (g) Asset   (h) Asset   (i) Asset   (j) Liability
(k) Asset   (l) Liability (m) Asset   (n) Liability (o) Asset
(p) Asset   (q) Assets   (r) Liability.

Answer 12

(a) Liability (b) Asset   c) Asset   (d) Liability (e) Asset
(f) Liability (g) Liability (h) Asset   (i) Liability,
(j) Asset   (k) Asset   (l) Asset   (m) Asset   (n) Asset
(o) Asset   (p) Asset   (q) Liability (r) Liability (s) Asset,
(t) Liability.

Answer 13

(a) £23,500,   (b) £16,430,   (c) £56,740

Answer 14

	Year 1	Year 2	Year 3	Year 4
Total Assets	22,500	6,230	11,000	47,333
Capital	22,500	6,230	11,000	47,333

Answer 15

	Year 1	Year 2	Year 3	Year 4
Net Assets	12,500	35,920	8,630	24,624
Capital	12,500	35,920	8,630	24,624

Answer 16

	Year 1	Year 2	Year 3	Year 4
Capital	13,560	18,139	25,659	34,179

Answer 17

	Year 1	Year 2	Year 3	Year 4
Capital	29,300	33,209	38,201	47,355

Answer 18

	Year 1	Year 2	Year 3	Year 4
Capital	11,600	12.030	12,950	13,660

Answer 19

a) Current Assets £10,000, (b) Capital £30,000,
(c) Current Liabilities £40,000, (d) Current Assets £25,000,
(e) Fixed Asset £31,000, (f) Current Liabilities £50,000,
(g) Capital £46,000, (h) Current Assets £39,000,
(i) Fixed Assets £40,000, (j) Current Assets £33,000.

Answer 20

(a) Net Assets £40,000,
(b) Net Assets £70,000,
(c) Net Assets £25,000,
(d)Current Assets £52,000,Net Assets £80,000,
(e) Capital £73,000,Net Assets £73,000
(f) Fixed Assets £40,000 Net Assets £45,000,
(g) Current Liabilities £38,000, Net Assets £54,000,
(h) Fixed Assets £85,000, Net Assets £90,000,
(i) Capital £48,000, Net Assets £48,000,
(j) Current Liabilities £13,000, Net Assets £46,000.

Answer 21

(a) Current Assets £30,000, Working Capital £10,000
(b) Capital £25,000, Working Capital (£3,000)
(c) Current Liabilities £5,000, Working Capital (£10,000)
(d) Capital £85,000, Working Capital £25,000
(e) Current Assets £22,000, Fixed Assets £23,000
(f) Capital £5,000, Working Capital (£10,000)
(g) Current Liabilities £11,000, Working Capital £3,000
(h) Current Assets £40,000, Working Capital £22,000
(i) Capital £70,000, Current Liabilities £15,000

Answer 22

Hotel

Capital	Revenue
Hotel	Heating and Lighting
Sports Equipment	Advertising
Computer Facilities	Cleaning Expenses

Sports Centre

Capital	Revenue
Sports Centre	Postage and Stationery
Gymnasium Equipment	Wages
Swimming Pool	Telephone Expenses

Leisure Park

Restaurant Facilities	Maintenance
Amusements	Power
Motor Vehicles	Rent and Rates

Car Factory

Factory	Factory Insurance
Plant and Machinery	Interest Payments
Fixtures and Fittings	Factory Power

Answer 23

(a) Revenue,   (b) Capital,   (c) Revenue,   (d) Capital,
(e) Revenue   (f) Capital,   (g) Revenue,   (h) Revenue,
(i) Revenue,   (j) Capital   (k) Capital,   (l) Revenue,
(m) Capital.

Note: Materiality concept must be applied in all cases.

Answer 24

(a) Capital ,	(b) Capital,	(c) Revenue,	(d) Capital,
(e) Capital,	(f) Capital,	(g) Capital,	(h) Revenue,
(i) Revenue,	(j) Capital,	(k) Revenue,	(l) Capital,
(m) Revenue,	(n) Capital,	(o) Capital,	(p) Revenue,
(r) Capital,	(s) Capital.		

Note: Materiality concept must always be applied.

Answer 25

(a) Expense,	(b) Asset,	(c) Liability,	(d) Expense,
(e) Expense	(f) Asset,	(g) Asset,	(h) Expense,
(i) Liability,	(j) Asset	(k) Asset,	(l) Asset,
(m) Expense,	(n) Liability,	(o) Expense,	(p) Asset,
(q) Liability,	(r) Liability,	(s) Expense	(t) Liability,
(u) Liability.			

Note: In some firms stationery may be shown as an asset if it has not been used at the end of the financial year.

Answer 26

(a) Trading Account,	(b) Trading Account,	(c) Profit and Loss,
(d) Profit and Loss,	(e) Profit and Loss,	(f) Profit and Loss,
(g) Trading Account,	(h) Trading Account,	(i) Profit and Loss,
(j) Trading Account,	(k) Profit and Loss,	(l) Profit and Loss,
(m) Trading Account,	(n) Profit and Loss,	(o) Profit and Loss.
(p) Trading Account,	(q) Profit and Loss,	(r) Profit and Loss.

Answer 27

(a) Trading Account,   (b) Trading Account,   (c) Trading Account,
(d) Trading Account,   (e) Profit and Loss.   (f) Trading Account,
(g) Trading Account,   (h) Profit and Loss,   (i) Profit and Loss,
(j) Profit and Loss,   (k) Profit and Loss,   (l) Profit and Loss,
(m) Profit and Loss,   (n) Profit and Loss,   (o) Profit and Loss,
(p) Profit and Loss,   (q) Profit and Loss,   (r) Profit and Loss

Answer 28

(a) Trading Account,   (b) Profit and Loss,   (c) Trading Account,
(d) Profit and Loss,   (e) Trading Account,   (f) Profit and Loss
(g) Profit and Loss,   (h) Profit and Loss,   (i) Trading Account,
(j) Profit and Loss,   (k) Profit and Loss,   (l) Profit and Loss,
(m) Trading Account,   (n) Profit and Loss,   (o) Profit and Loss,
(p) Profit and Loss,   (q) Trading Account,   (r) Profit and Loss,
(s) Profit and Loss.

Answer 29

(a) Income,   (b) Expense,   (c) Liability,
(d) Expense,   (e) Asset,   (f) Income,
(g) Income,   (h) Liability,   (i) Asset
(j) Expense,   (k) Liability,   (l) Expense,
(m) Income,   (n) Expense,   (o) Expense,
(p) Expense,   (q) Liability,   (r) Asset,
(s) Asset,   (t) Asset,   (u) Income.

Answer 30

(a) Balance Sheet,   (b) Trading Account,   (c) Profit and Loss
(d) Profit and Loss and Balance Sheet,   (e) Balance Sheet
(f) Trading Account,   (g) Profit and Loss,   (h) Balance Sheet
(i) Balance Sheet,   (j) Balance Sheet,   (k) Trading Account,
(l) Trading Account and Balance Sheet,   (m) Profit and Loss,
(n) Trading Account,   (o) Balance Sheet,   (p) Profit and Loss,
(q) Balance Sheet,   (r) Balance Sheet,   (s) Balance Sheet,
(t) Balance Sheet,   (u) Trading Account.

Answer 31

(a) Trading Account,   (b) Profit and Loss,   (c) Profit and Loss,
(d) Profit and Loss,   (e) Balance Sheet,   (f) Profit and Loss,
(g) Balance Sheet,   (h) Profit and Loss,   (i) Profit and Loss,
(j) Balance Sheet,   (k) Balance Sheet,   (l) Balance Sheet,
(m) Profit and Loss,   (n) Balance Sheet,   (o) Profit and Loss,
(p) Balance Sheet,   (q) Balance Sheet,   (r) Balance Sheet,
(s) Profit and Loss.

Answer 32

Gross Profit	Year 1	Year 2	Year 3	Year 4
	£	£	£	£
	19,500	23,500	14,832	32,090

Answer 33

	Year 1	Year 2	Year 3	Year 4
	£	£	£	£
Gross Profit	7,880	42,101	43,585	23,561

Answer 34

Firm's Trading Account For The Year Ending 5 April Year One

	£	£
Sales		36,700
Opening Stock	5,832	
Add Purchases	23,800	
	29,632	
Less Closing Stock	3,100	
Cost of Goods Sold		26,532
Gross Profit		10,168

Answer 35

Firm's Trading Account For The Year Ending 5 April Year One

	£	£
Sales		25,100
Less Returns Inwards		750
Net Sales		24,350
Opening Stock	2,300	
Add Purchases	11,400	
Add Carriage Inwards	430	
	14,130	
Less Closing Stock	1,500	
Cost of Goods Sold		12,630
Gross Profit		11,720

Answer 36

Firm's Trading Account For The Year Ending 5 April Year One

	£	£	£
Sales			65,700
Opening Stock		7,420	
Add Purchases	22,490		
Less Returns Outwards	3,200		
Net Purchases		19,290	
Add Carriage Inwards		1,398	
		28,108	
Less Closing Stock		4,567	
Cost of Goods Sold			23,541
Gross Profit			42,159

Answer 37

Firm's Profit and Loss Account For The Year Ending 5 April Year One.

	£	£
Gross Profit		23,500
Discount Received		300
		23,800
Less Expenses:		
Rent	500	
Wages	2,000	
Insurance	700	
Telephone and Postage	800	
Depreciation	900	
Total Expenses		4,900
Gross Profit		18,900

Answer 38

(a) Capital,   (b) Debtor,   (c) Carriage Inwards,
(d) Discount Allowed,   (e) Returns Outwards, (f) Creditor,
(g) Prepayment   (h) Discount Received, (i) Carriage Outwards,
(j) Work in progress.

Answer 39 The Confectionery Store

Balance Sheet 5 April Year One

Fixed Assets	£	£
Shop lease		17,000
Delivery Van		4,000
Current Assets		
Stock		18,000
Debtors		500
Cash		8,000
		47,500
Less Liabilities		
Creditors	3,000	
Bank Loan	3,000	
		6,000
Net Assets		41,500

Answer 40 - The Flower Shop

Balance Sheet of the Flower Shop as at 5th April Year One

Fixed Assets

	£	£
Premises		10,000
Fixtures and Fittings		5,000
Motor Vehicles		4,000
		19,000

Current Assets

Stock	2,000	
Debtors	4,000	
Bank	2,500	
Cash	500	
	9,000	

Current Liabilities

Creditors	5,000	
Working Capital		4,000
Net Assets		23,000
Capital		
Owner's Equity	20,000	
Profits	7,000	
	27,000	
Less Drawings	4,000	
Capital Employed		23,0000

Net Assets are calculated by subtracting the firm's liabilities from the total of the fixed and current assets. As a result the net assets figure must equal capital.

Answer 41 - New Ventures

a) Fixed assets are long term assets used for trading. Simon's business only has one fixed asset and that is his premises.

b) Working capital is calculated by subtracting current liabilities form a firm's current assets. Simon's working capital is:

Current Assets

	£
Stock	28,020
Debtors	19,260
Bank	11,220
	58,500
Current Liabilities	
Creditors	25,860
Working Capital	32,640

c) Net Assets = Fixed Assets plus Current Assets less Liabilities.
   Net Assets £38,700
   Note: Bank Term Loan is not a current liability.

d) Capital Employed = Net Assets £38,700

Answer 42 - Mountain Biker

Trading Profit and Loss Account for Mountain Biker For The Year Ending 31 March Year One.

	£	£
Sales		60,000
Purchases	35,500	
Less Closing Stock	7,000	
Cost of Goods Sold		28,500
Gross Profit		31,500
Less Expenses:		
Wages	10,000	
Lighting and Heating	3,000	
Postage and Telephone	1,500	
Cleaning	1,000	
Motor Expenses	700	
Repairs to Shop	500	
General Expenses	800	
Total Expenses		17,500
Gross Profit		14,000

Answer 43 - Gardens and Lawns

Trading, Profit and Loss Account and Balance Sheet For Gardens and Lawns For The Year Ending 5 April Year One.

	£	£
Sales		101,160
Add Purchases	54,225	
Less Closing Stock	13,275	
Cost of Goods Sold		40,950
Gross Profit		60,210
Less Expenses:		
Wages	31,230	
Office Expenses	4,410	
Motor Expenses	2,565	
Office Cleaning	855	
Advertising	2,025	
Insurance	1,125	
Total Expenses		42,210
Net Profit		18,000

Balance Sheet as at 5 April Year One.

Capital		Fixed Assets	
	£	£	
Capital	20,000		
Add Profit	18,000		
Current Liabilities		**Current Assets**	
Creditors	14,445	Stock	13,275
Bank Overdraft	7,000	Debtors	46,170
	59,445		59,445

Answer 44 - Master Crafts

Trading, Profit and Loss Account and Balance Sheet For Master Crafts For The Year Ending 31 March Year 8.

	£	£
Sales		56,200
Opening Stock	8,150	
Add Purchases	21,000	
Add Carriage Inwards	975	
	30,125	
Less Closing Stock	7,375	
Cost of Goods Sold		22,750
Gross Profit		33,450
Less Expenses:		
Wages	17,350	
Advertising	2,000	
Carriage Outwards	175	
Rent	3,625	
Total Expenses		23,150
Net Profit		10,300

Balance Sheet as at 31 March Year 8

Capital	£	Fixed Assets	£
Capital	10,000		
Add Profit	10,300		
Current Liabilities		Current Assets	
Creditors	8,025	Stock	7,375
Bank Loan	5,000	Debtors	19,725
		Bank	6,225
	33,325		33,325

Note: Prepayment increases debtors by £300 and reduces rent by £300.

Answer 45 - Travel There

Trading Profit and Loss Account For The Year Ending 5 April Year One.

	£	£
Commission Income		38,765
Add Discount Received		450
		39,215
Less Expenses:		
Bank Interest Paid	130	
Rent	9,768	
Wages	21,016	
Heating	876	
Office Stationery	300	
Office Sundries	100	
Postage and Telephone	2,739	
Travelling Expenses	76	
Leasing Payments	330	
Discount Allowed	880	
Cleaning	2,400	
Total Expenses		38,615
Net Profit		600

Note: In the Profit and Loss Account amounts owing (accruals) are added and amounts prepaid are deducted.

Answer 46 - Hutton's Shoe Shop

Trading, Profit and Loss Account and Balance Sheet For The Year Ending 5 April Year Two.

	£	£
Sales		73,848
Opening Stock	12,996	
Add Purchases	45,520	
	58,516	
Less Closing Stock	10,192	
Cost of Goods Sold		48,324
Gross Profit		25,524

Less Expenses:

	£	£
Wages	8,600	
Lighting and Heating	10,750	
Insurance	444	
General Expenses	370	
Total Expenses		20,164
Net Profit		5,360

Balance Sheet as at 5 April Year Two

Capital	£	Fixed Assets	£
Capital	17,696	Fixtures and Fittings	4,800
Add Profit	5,360		
	23,056		
Less Drawings	6,356		
	16,700		
Current Liabilities		**Current Assets**	
Creditors	6,302	Stock	10,192
Bank Loan	3,840	Debtors	7,850
		Cash	4,000
	26,842		26,842

Note: Lighting owing added to creditors and general expenses prepaid added to debtors

Answer 47 - Harry's Pet Shop

Trading, Profit and Loss Account For The Year Ending 31 December Year Four.

	£	£
Sales		187,320
Less Returns Inwards		2,700
Net Sales		184,620
Opening Stock	32,490	
Add Purchases	113,800	
	146,290	
Less Closing Stock	25,480	
Cost of Goods Sold		120,810
Gross Profit		63,810
Less Expenses:		
Wages	21,500	
Lighting and Heating	26,500	
Carriage Outwards	6,000	
Motor Repairs	1,110	
Sundry Expenses	1,050	
Total Expenses		56,160
Net Profit		7,650

Balance Sheet as at 31 December Year Four.

Capital		Fixed Assets	
	£		£
Capital	38,940	Motor Vehicles	12,000
Add Profit	7,650		
	46,590		
Less Drawings	15,390		
	31,200		
Current Liabilities		Current Assets	
Creditors	18,380	Stock	25,480
Loan	3,000	Debtors	19,500
Bank Overdraft	2,300	Cash	10,500
Bank Loan	12,600		
	67,480		67,480

Answer 48 - Electrical Wholesalers Limited

Balance Sheet as at 5 April Year 7.

Capital	£	Fixed Assets	£
Share Capital	300,000	Goodwill	20,000
Share Premium	15,000	Premises	296,000
General Reserve	5,000	Fixtures & Fittings	95,830
Debentures	155,000	Motor Vehicles	32,560
Current Liabilities		Current Assets	
Creditors	109,990	Stock	68,450
		Debtors	59,200
		Bank	12,950
	584,990		584,990

Answer 49 - Spark of Life

Trading, Profit and Loss Account and Balance Sheet for Spark of Life For The Year Ending 31st September Year Five.

	£	£
Sales		189,423
Opening Stock	14,787	
Add Purchases	113,602	
Add Carriage Inwards	8,901	
	137,290	
Less Closing Stock	20,045	
Cost of Goods Sold		117,245
Gross Profit		72,178
Commission Received		2,702
		74,880
Less Expenses:		
Insurance	24,256	
Carriage Outwards	3,402	
Discount Allowed	3,954	
Wages	20,630	
Directors' Emoluments	15,201	
Advertising	3,400	
Rent and Rates	11,982	
Total Expenses		82,825
Loss		7,945

Spark of Life
Balance Sheet as at 31 September Year Five

	£	£
Fixed Assets		
Goodwill		25,000
Motor Vehicles		16,520
Current Assets		
Stock	20,045	
Debtors	13,807	
Investments	4,000	
Bank	13,920	
	51,772	
Less Liabilities		
Creditors	6,237	
Working Capital		45,535
Net Assets		87,055
Capital		
70,000 Ord £1 Shares		70,000
Revaluation Reserve		15,000
General Reserve		10,000
Profit and Loss		(7.945)
Shareholders' Funds		87,055

Answer 50

Please see appendix for the correct layout

Answer 51 - The General Trading Company Limited

INCOME

a) Turnover
b) Income from investments
c) Rental income received
d) Profit or loss on the sale of fixed assets

EXPENSES

a) Staff costs
b) Directors' emoluments
c) Employees' emoluments
d) Interest payments
e) Hire of plant
f) Auditing fees
g) Depreciation
h) Reduction in the value of investments

Appropriation of Profit

a) Taxation
b) Reduction in goodwill
c) Transfers to reserves
d) Dividends Paid

Answer 52 - Plumbing Supplies Limited

Value Added Statement for Plumbing Supplies Limited for the 31st March Year 4.

	£
Sales	324,000
Less: Cost of Goods Sold	120,500
Value added by the company	203,500
To Employees:	
Wages and Benefits	75,000
To Providers of Capital:	
Interest	14,000
Dividends	22,000
To Government:	
Taxation	40,000
To Finance & Maintain Fixed Assets:	
Depreciation	17,000
Retained Profit	35,000
Value Added	203,000

Answer 53 - Executive Stationery Supplies

a) A van is a fixed asset which will have a working life of several years and so it would be wrong to write the cost off the van against one years profit.

b) Historical Cost Concept and the Going Concern Concept. Assets are shown at their cost price rather than their current market value because there is an assumption that they will be used for several years.

c) The legal cost is part of the cost of acquiring the premises and so the cost is treated as capital expenditure and shown in the balance sheet rather than treating it as revenue expenditure.

Answer 54 - Road Hauliers

a) The term residual value means the estimated value of a fixed asset once it has reached the end of its working life. The figure can only be an estimate because the precise value of any asset is only known once it has been sold. Nevertheless, by estimating a residual value the cost of the asset can be spread by means of depreciation charges over the working life of the asset.

b) The depreciation charge will generally not equal the asset's fall in market value. The aim is to spread the cost of the asset over its working life and not to provide for the asset's loss in market value.

c)

Fixed Assets	£
Truck	40,000
Less Residual Value	4,000
	36,000
Estimated Working Life	6 Years

Depreciation £6,000

Extract of Balance Sheet as at Year One

Fixed Asset	Cost	Depreciation	Net Book Value
	£	£	£
Truck	40,000	6,000	34,000

Answer 55

a)	Premises	£143,000
b)	Fixtures	£40,000
c)	Motor Van	£6,000

Answer 56

Depreciation provision for each year £10,000

Extract of Balance Sheet as at Year One

Fixed Asset	Cost £	Depreciation £	Net Book Value £
Computer	50,000	10,000	40,000
Year Two Computer	50,000	20,000	30,000
Year Three Computer	50,000	30,000	20,000
Year Four Computer	50,000	40,000	10,000
Year Five Computer	50,000	50,000	Nil

Answer 57

Cost of Lorry £85,000

Extract of Balance Sheet as at Year One

Fixed Asset	Cost £	Depreciaton £	Net Book Value £
Year One Lorry	85,000	12,750	72,250
Year Two Lorry	85,000	23,588	61,412
Year Three Lorry	85,000	32,800	52,200
Year Four Lorry	85,000	40,630	44,370
Year Five Lorry	85,000	47,286	37,714

Note: All figures to nearest whole number.

Answer 58

Extract of Balance Sheet as at Year One

Fixed Assets

Extract of Balance Sheet as at Year One

Fixed Assets	Cost	Depreciation to Date	Net Book Value
	£	£	£
Year One			
Motor Van	12,000	2,400	9,600
Computer	3,000	750	2,250
Year Two			
Motor Van	12,000	4,800	7,200
Computer	3,000	1,500	1,500
Year Three			
Motor Van	12,000	7,200	4,800
Computer	3,000	2,250	750

Answer 59

	£
Cost of Electric Saw	10,000
Less Residual Value	2,000
	8,000

Cost/Hours £8,000/60,000 hours

Depreciation charge per hour 13p (approx)

Answer 60

	£
Cost of Chair Lift	100,000
Less Residual Value	3,000
	97,000

Cost/Hours £97,000/350,000 hours

Depreciation charge per hour 28p (approx)

Answer 61

	£
Cost of Carpet	60,000
Expected Life	3,600 days

Cost/Days £60,000/3,600 days

Depreciation charge per day   £16.66

Answer 62

	£
Cost of Truck	85,000
Less Residual Value	5,950
	79,050

Cost/Miles £79,050/250,000

Depreciation charge per mile 32p (approx)

Answer 63

	£
Cost of Machine	20,000
Less Residual Value	1,500
	18,500

Cost/Units £18,500/50,000

Depreciation charge per unit 37p

Answer 64

	£
Cost of machine	10,000
Residual Value	—
	10,000

Cost/ Units £10,000/30,000

Depreciation charge per unit 33p (approx)

Answer 65

	£
Cost of Deep Freeze	4,000
Residual Value	—
	4,000

Cost/Days £4,000/1825

Depreciation charge per day £2.19

Answer 66 - European Hauliers

(a) £5,000;   (b) £6,500;   (c) £7,500;   (d) £4,000;
(e) £5,000;   (f) £4,250;   (g) £17,000;   (h) £9,333;
(i) £1,625;   (j) £2,350   (k) £2614.

Answer 67 - Plant Hauliers

Reducing Balance

	Cost £	Dep. Rate %	Yr. One £	Yr. Two £	Yr. Three £
a)	30,000	12	3,600	3,168	2,788
b)	47,000	10	4,700	4,230	3,807
c)	12,000	20	2,400	1,920	1,536
d)	28,000	15	4,200	3,570	3,035
e)	60,000	25	15,000	11,250	8,438
f)	25,000	14	3,500	3,010	2,589
g)	10,000	5	500	475	451
h)	40,000	14	5,600	4,816	4,142

Note: All numbers to nearest whole number.

Straight Line

	Cost £	Dep. Rate. %	Yr. One £	Yr. Two £	Yr. Three £
a)	30,000	12	3,600	3,600	3,600
b)	47,000	10	4,700	4,700	4,700
c)	12,000	20	2,400	2,400	2,400
d)	28,000	15	4,200	4,200	4,200
e)	60,000	25	15,000	15,000	15,000
f)	25,000	14	3,500	3,500	3,500
g)	10,000	5	500	500	500
h)	40,000	14	5,600	5,600	5,600

Answer 68 - Zolan Limited

(a)

	50%	60%	70%	80%	90%	100%
	£	£	£	£	£	£
Materials	60,000	72,000	84,000	96,000	108,000	120,000
Labour	40,000	48,000	56,000	64,000	72,000	80,000
Var. Oh'ds	15,000	18,000	21,000	24,000	27,000	30,000
Fixed Costs	40,000	40,000	40,000	40,000	40,000	40,000
Total Cost	155,000	178,000	201,000	224,000	247,000	270,000

(b) Selling Price Less Variable Cost = Contribution

	£	£
Selling Price		17.00
Less Variable Costs		
Materials	6	
Labour	4	
Variable Overheads	1.50	
		11.50
Contribution		5.50

(c) Contribution x Output = Total Contribution Less Fixed Costs Equals Profit.

Output Units	Total Contribution £	Fixed Costs £	Profit £
10,000	55,000	40,000	15,000
12,000	66,000	40,000	26,000
14,000	77,000	40,000	37,000
16,000	88,000	40,000	48,000
18,000	99,000	40,000	59,000
20,000	110,000	40,000	70,000

Answer 69 - Zoraq Limited

Output	Fixed Cost £	Variable Cost £	Sales £	Profit £
1,000	20,000	3,000	8,000	(15,000)
2,000	20,000	6,000	16,000	(10,000)
3,000	20,000	9,000	24,000	(5,000)
4,000	20,000	12,000	32,000	Break Even
5,000	20,000	15,000	40,000	5,000
6,000	20,000	18,000	48,000	10,000
7,000	20,000	21,000	56,000	15,000
8,000	20,000	24,000	64,000	20,000
9,000	20,000	27,000	72,000	25,000
10,000	20,000	30,000	80,000	30,000
11,000	20,000	33,000	88,000	35,000
12,000	20,000	36,000	96,000	40,000
13,000	20,000	39,000	104,000	45,000
14,000	20,000	42,000	112,000	50,000
15,000	20,000	45,000	120,000	55,000

Note ( ) mean a loss

Answer 70 - Markan Limited

Output	Sales £	Fixed Costs £	Variable Costs £	Profit £
1,000	65,000	30,000	25,000	10,000
2,000	130,000	30,000	50,000	50,000
3,000	195,000	30,000	75,000	90,000
4,000	260,000	30,000	100,000	130,000
5,000	325,000	30,000	125,000	170,000
6,000	390,000	30,000	150,000	210,000
7,000	455,000	30,000	175,000	250,000
8,000	520,000	30,000	200,000	290,000
9,000	585,000	30,000	225,000	330,000

Answer 71 - The Electric Motor Company

Output Per Month	Total Fixed Cost	Fixed Cost Per Unit	Total Variable Cost	Variable Cost Per Unit
	£	£	£	£
0	250,000	250,000	—	—
500	250,000	500	39,000	78
1,000	250,000	250	78,000	78
3,000	250,000	83	234,000	78
6,000	250,000	42	468,000	78
10,000	250,000	25	780,000	78
15,000	250,000	17	1,170,000	78
30,000	250,000	8	2,340,000	78
45,000	250,000	6	3,510,000	78
50,000	250,000	5	3,900,000	78
60,000	250,000	4	4,680,000	78

Note: Numbers to the nearest £.

Answer 72

Materials - Direct;
Direct;
Cleansing Materials - Indirect;
Rates - Indirect.

Rent - Indirect; Direct Labour
Supervisors' Wages - Indirect;
Factory Insurance - Indirect;

Note: If cleansing materials are significant to the task being undertaken they might be treated as a direct cost.

Answer 73

The variable cost for Product X is always £5.40 regardless of the level of output.

Answer 74

The material cost for Product Y is £2.25 regardless of the level of output.

Answer 75

The direct labour cost of Product Z is £6.30 regardless of the level of output

Answer 76

The fixed costs at half operating capacity will be £10,000.

Fixed costs per unit at the following levels of output;

Output	Fixed Cost Per Unit
1	£10,000
100	£100
200	£50
300	£33
400	£25
500	£20
600	£16.66
700	£14.28
800	£12.50
900	£11.11
1,000	£10.00

Answer 77

£15,000;   £16,000;   £5,900;   £22,000   £23,700

Answer 78

£45,000;   £31,000;   £8,000;   £11,000   £7,000

Answer 79

£7.57;   £8.50;   £12.83;   £14.05:   £27.10

Answer 80

£4.00

Answer 81

The unit variable cost will always be £5.00

Answer 82

£500;   £1,000;   £1,500;   £2,000

Answer 83

£8.00;   £7.99;   _   £3.00;   £6.00

Answer 84

50%;   33.3%;   28%;   20%

Answer 85

9,000 units;   3,000 units;   3,000 units;   4,000 units

Answer 86

Contribution £40,000; £40,000;   £40,000;   £61,000;
Break Even £22,500;   £34,375;   £60,000;   £51,639

Answer 87

£17,600;   £55,000;   £56,000;   £33,000

Answer 88

Product D.

Answer 89

Contribution earned Product A £6; Product B£5; Product C£7; Product D £9. Always make the one which makes the largest contribution which in this case is Product D.

Answer 90 - Monal

| Overhead | Basis of Apportionment | Cost Centres | | | Total |
		EC1 £	EC2 £	EC3 £	£
Rent	Area	4,200	3,800	2,000	10,000
Rates	Area	1,890	1,710	900	4,500
Power	Machine Hours	4.050	2,970	1,980	9,000
Supervision	No. Of Employees	9,120	4,640	2,240	16,000
Heating	Area	1,680	1,520	800	4,000
Depreciation	Value of Plant	1,197	609	294	2,100

Answer 91 - Trees and Shrubs

| Overhead | Basis of Apportionment | Cost Centres | | | Total |
		EC1 £	EC2 £	EC3 £	£
Rent	Area	5,100	9,900	15,000	30,000
Rates	Area	1,360	2,640	4,000	8,000
Power	Machine Hours	2,550	4,950	7,500	15,000
Supervision	No. Of Employees	6,000	7,920	10,080	24,000
Heating	Area	5,100	9,900	15,000	30,000
Depreciation	Value of Plant	1,120	2,320	4,560	8,000
Insurance	Value of Stock	5,900	2,900	1,200	10,000

Answer 92 - Adventure Parks Limited

Effective Machine Hours:

360 days x 10 hours =	3,600 hours
Less 10% idle time =	360 hours
	3,240

Total Annual Cost:

	£
Annual Overhead	2,000
Operators' Wages	
(360 days x 10 hours x £5)	18,000
Power	
(3,240 hours x £1)	3,240
	23,240

$$\frac{\text{Cost} \quad £23,240}{\text{Hours} \quad 3,240} = £7.17 \text{ per hour}$$

Answer 93 - Harvest Pies

Effective Hours:

261 days x 7 hours =	1,827	hours
Less 5% idle time	91	hours
	1,736	hours

	£
Total Annual Cost	
Annual Overhead	2,900
Operators' Wages	
(261 days x 7 hours x £3)	5,481
Power	
(1736 hours x 50p)	868
	9,249

$$\frac{\text{Cost} \quad £9,249}{\text{Hours} \quad 1,736} = £5.33 \text{ per hour}$$

Note: All numbers rounded to nearest whole number.

Answer 94 - Hi Slope Skis

	October £	November £	December £
Materials	255,000	289,000	340,000
Output	15,000	17,000	20,000
Cost Per Unit	17	17	17
Labour	180,000	204,000	240,000
Output	15,000	17,000	20,000
Cost Per Unit	12	12	12

Calculation of Variable Overhead

	Cost £	Activity £
Highest	113,500	20,000
Lowest	93,500	15,000
Change in Cost/Activity	20,000	5,000

$$\frac{\text{Cost £20,000}}{\text{Activity 5,000}} = £4$$

Therefore, variable cost of overhead is £4 per unit.

Calculation of Fixed Cost of Overhead:

	October £	November £	December £
Total Overhead	93,500	101,500	113,500
Variable O'hd			
£4 x output	60,000	68,000	80,000
Fixed Cost	33,500	33,500	33,500

(a) Unit Variable Cost of Manufacturing Skis.

	£
Materials	17
Labour	12
Variable O'hd	4
	33

(b) Output x unit variable cost plus fixed cost.

$$25,000 \quad x \quad £33 \quad = \quad £825,000 \quad + \quad £33,500 \quad = \quad £858,500$$

(c) Break Even

	October	November	December
	£	£	£
Fixed Costs	33,500	33,500	33,500
Contribution	20	20	20
Break-even Point-Units	1,675	1,675	1,675

Answer 95 - Bridge Hotel

	Jan. £	Feb. £	March. £	April. £	May. £
Food	94,800	118,500	156,420	189,600	213,300
Output	20,000	25,000	33,000	40,000	45,000
Cost Per Meal	£4.74	£4.74	£4.74	£4.74	£4.74
Labour	25,800	32,250	42,570	51,600	58,050
Output	20,000	25,000	33,000	40,000	45,000
Cost Per Meal	£1.29	£1.29	£1.29	£1.29	£1.29

Calculation of Variable Overhead

	Cost £	Activity
Highest	129,150	45,000
Lowest	82,400	20,000
	46,750	25,000

$$\frac{\text{Cost}}{\text{Activity}} = \frac{£46,750}{25,000} = £1.87$$

Therefore, variable cost of overhead is £1.87 per meal.

Calculation of Fixed Overhead:

	Jan. £	Feb. £	March. £	April. £	May. £
Overhead	82,400	91,750	106,710	119,800	129,150
Variable					
O'hd x Output	37,400	46,750	61,710	74,800	84,150
Fixed Cost	45,000	45,000	45,000	45,000	45,000

(a) Variable Costs of the Restaurant

	£
Food	4.74
Labour	1.29
Variable Overhead	1.87
Total Variable Unit Cost	7.90

(b) Fixed Costs £45,000 per month

(c) Contribution = Selling Price less Variable Cost.

	£
Selling Price Per Meal	12.50
Less Variable Cost	7.90
Contribution Per Meal	4.60

(d) Break even = Fixed Costs divided by contribution.

$$\frac{\text{Fixed Costs} \quad £45{,}000}{\text{Contribution} \quad £4.60} = 9783 \text{ meals to break even}$$

Answer 96 - Leaded Lights

	May. £	June. £	July. £	Aug. £	Sept. £	Oct. £
Glass	4,500	5,580	6,300	7,560	8,100	8,460
Units	500	620	700	840	900	940
Cost per unit	9	9	9	9	9	9
Labour	2,315	2,871	3,241	3,889	4,167	4,352
Units	500	620	700	840	900	940
Cost per unit	£4.63	£4.63	£4.63	£4.63	£4.63	£4.63

Calculation of Variable Overhead:

	Cost £	Output
Highest	12,416	940
Lowest	11,285	500
	1,131	440

$$\frac{\text{Cost} \quad £1,131}{\text{Activity} \quad 440} = £2.57$$

Therefore, Variable cost of overhead per unit is £2.57

Calculation of Fixed Overhead

	May. £	June. £	July. £	Aug. £	Sept. £	Oct. £
Overhead	11,285	11,593	11,799	12,159	12,313	12,416
Variable Cost per unit x output	1,285	1,593	1,799	2,159	2,313	2,416
Fixed Cost	10,000	10,000	10,000	10,000	10,000	10,000

(a) Variable Cost   £

      Glass   9.00

      Labour   4.63

      Variable Overhead   2.57

      Unit Variable Cost   16.20

(b) Fixed Costs £10,000 per month.

172

Answer 97 - Geoff's Garage

(a) Break even is the term used by accountants to describe the point where total sales equal total costs. At this level of sales the firm makes neither a profit or loss but merely covers its costs.

(b) Calculation of Break Even Point

	£	£
Selling Price		14.50
Less Variable Costs:		
Oil	5.00	
Filter	3.50	
		8.50
Contribution		6.00

Calculation of Fixed Costs	£
Ramp	1,000
Wages	12,000
Overheads	7,000
Total Fixed Costs	20,000

$$\text{Break Even} = \frac{\text{Fixed Costs}}{\text{Contribution}} = \frac{£20,000}{£6} = 3,333 \text{ services to break-even.}$$

Answer 98 - Watch Straps

(a) Marginal cost per watch strap £2

(b) Contribution from each sale £10

(c) Contribution earned for

January	£60,000
February	£85,000
March	£94,000

Answer 99 - Down at Heel

(a) Contribution per shoe

Men's	£1.50
Women's	£1.30
Children	55p

(b) Contribution per unit x output = total contribution less fixed costs = Profit.

			£
Men's	30,000 x £1.50	=	45,000
Women's	40,000 x £1.30	=	52,000
Children's	30,000 x £0.55	=	16,500
Total Contribution			113,500
Less Fixed Costs:		£	
Rent		25,000	
Insurance		3,000	
Leasing Costs		6,000	
			34,000
Profit			79,500

(c) Men's shoes because it has the highest contribution.

174

Answer 100 - The Potter's Wheel

(a)   Marginal cost - Small £3.25; Medium £4.35; Large £6.00

(b)   Contribution - Small £3.75; Medium £4.65; Large £5.00

(c)   In the absence of any other constraints the firm should make the
       product which will yield the greatest contribution. This can be
       calculated by dividing the time to make each pot into the
       contribution earned from each sale.

	Small £	Medium £	Large £
Contribution	3.75	4.65	5.00
Time (hours)	2	3	4
Contribution per hour	£1.88	£1.55	£1.25

The firm should make the small pot because it makes the largest
contribution.

Answer 101 - Tailored Suits

(a) Grey £35; Brown £45; Blue £35

(b) Grey £105,000; Brown £45,000; Blue £175,000
Total Contribution £325,000

(c) Brown

Answer 102 - River Craft

		RC1 £		RC2 £		RC3 £
Selling Price		250		400		375
Less Variable Costs:	£		£		£	
Materials	85		149		120	
Labour	65		180		90	
Variable Cost		150		329		210
Contribution		100		71		165
Hours		20		25		22
Contribution Per Hour		£5		£2.84		£7.50

The company should make model RC3 because it earns the greatest contribution from each hour earned.

Answer 103 - Smithdown Stores

Department	Contribution £	Fixed Cost £	Profit £
Mens	33,000	25,000	8,000
Womens	70,000	40,000	30,000
Furniture	18,000	20,000	(2,000)
Hair Salon	28,000	10,000	18,000
Restaurant	35,000	15,000	20,000
Electrical	25,000	25,000	B/Even
Current Profit			74,000

Proposal Close Furniture Department and Let Out Space:

Rental Income	£40,000
Less Fixed Costs	£20,000
Additional Profit	20,000

New Profit £76,000   +   £20,000   =   £96,000

Increase in profit £22,000.

Answer 104 - Metal Forge masters

(a)   Marginal Cost: £
      Direct Materials   200
      Direct Labour   75
      Variable Overheads   30
                                              305

(b)
                                              £
      Selling Price   630
      Less Variable Costs   305
      Contribution   325

(c)   Break Even:

      Fixed Costs   £25,000
      ───────────────────────────── = 77 units
      Contribution   £325

Note: Break even to nearest whole number.

Answer 105 - Carpets and Curtains

	Job A £		Job B £
Selling Price	1,400		1,200
Less Variable Costs:	£		£
Direct materials	600		460
Labour	200		170
Direct expenses	50		80
Variable Cost		850	710
Contribution		550	490
Less Fixed Costs		400	340
Profit		150	150

From the information given Emma should subcontract Job B because it makes a smaller contribution.

Note: In such a case it would be useful to know the method employed for apportioning overheads.

Answer 106 - Southern Cross Hotel

	Docklands £	City £	Waterside £
Sales	80,000	150,000	197,000
Less Variable Costs:			
Food	25,000	45,000	63,000
Labour	25,000	35,000	45,000
Variable O'hd	12,000	12,000	12,000
Total Variable Cost	62,000	92,000	120,000
Contribution	18,000	58,000	77,000
Less F. Costs	28,000	28,000	28,000
Profit/(Loss)	(10,000)	30,000	49,000

Total Profit £79,000 Less £10,000 Loss = £69,000.

Proposal to Close the Docklands Restaurant:

	£
Contribution	135,000
Less Fixed Costs	84,000
Profit	51,000

£18,000 reduction in profit because in the short term the hotel still has to meet the fixed costs.

Note: In the short term so long as a department or product makes a contribution towards fixed costs it should be kept.

Answer 107 - Central Theme Parks

Attraction	Shark £	Swamp £	Tunnel £
Sales	130,000	90,000	225,000
Less Variable Costs:			
Variable Costs	50,000	35,000	70,000
Direct Labour	35,000	15,000	40,000
Total Variable Cost	85,000	50,000	110,000
Contribution	45,000	40,000	115,000
Less Fixed Costs	65,000	20,000	55,000
Profit/(loss)	(20,000)	20,000	60,000

Profit £60,000

Proposal to Close Shark Ride:

	£
Contribution	155,000
Less Fixed Costs	140,000
Pofit	15,000

Closure would reduce profits by £45,000.

Answer 108 - Leather Crafts

Spanish Order:

	£	£
Selling Price		72
Less Variable Costs:		
Materials	40	
Labour	25	
		65
Contribution		7

Total Contribution = Unit Contribution x Output

$$£7 \times 425 = £2,975$$

	£	£
Selling Price		120
Less Variable Costs:		
Materials	40	
Labour	25	
		65
Contribution		55

Total Contribution = Unit Contribution x Output

$$£55 \times 425 = £23,375$$

	£
Contribution From Spanish Order	2,975
Contribution From Other Orders	23,375
Total Contribution	26,350
Less Fixed Costs	24,000
Profit	2,350

Accept Order

Answer 109 - Leisure Cruises

Product	Dh1	Dh2	Dh3
	£	£	£
Sales	150,000	200,000	75,000
Less Variable Costs:			
Materials	47,000	60,000	35,000
Labour	50,000	70,000	40,000
Variable Overhead	4,000	6,000	2,000
Total Variable Cost	101,000	136,000	77,000
Contribution	49,000	64,000	(2,000)
Less Fixed Costs	16,000	24,000	8,000
Profit/(Loss)	33,000	40,000	(10,000)

If Product Abandoned:

	£
Total Contribution	113,000
Less Fixed Costs	48,000
Profit	65,000

Recommendation: Stop making Product Dh3 because the selling price does not cover the variable costs of manufacture.

(b) In the short term the business must pay its fixed costs. As a result any contribution which can be earned will go towards meeting fixed costs. In this case product Dh3 does not earn any contribution and therefore, makes no money which can be used to meet fixed costs. It should therefore, be abandoned.

Answer 110 - The South West Brewing Company

Flexible Budget for South West Brewing Company

Activity	70%	80%	90%	100%
	£	£	£	£
Rent	70,000	70,000	70,000	70,000
Rates	15,000	15,000	15,000	15,000
Prime Cost	63,000	72,000	81,000	90,000
Insurance	10,000	10,000	10,000	10,000
Indirect Labour	20,000	20,000	20,000	20,000
Advertising	5,000	5,000	5,000	5,000
Total Cost	183,000	192,000	201,000	210,000

Note: The company has high fixed costs and these remain fixed regardless of the level of activity.

Answer 111 - The Wooden Fencing Company

Activity	70%	80%	90%	100%	110%
	£	£	£	£	£
Rent	100,000	100,000	100,000	100,000	100,000
Rates	20,000	20,000	20,000	20,000	20,000
D.Materials	420,000	480,000	540,000	600,000	660,000
D.Labour	315,000	360,000	405,000	450,000	495,000
Power	84,000	96,000	108,000	120,000	132,000
Insurance	20,000	20,000	20,000	20,000	20,000
I. Labour	30,000	30,000	30,000	30,000	30,000
Total Cost	989,000	1,110,600	1,122,300	1,134,000	1,457,000

Answer 112 - R and H Metal Manufacturers

	£	£
Sales		948,300
Less Variable Costs:		
Raw Materials	162,750	
Wages	139,100	
Variable Overheads	39,220	
Total Variable Cost		341,070
Contribution		607,230
Less Fixed Costs		50,440
Profit		556,790

Answer 113 - The Malaysian Restaurant

(a)

	£	£
Sales		112,000
Less Variable Costs:		
Food	31,200	
Wages	26,525	
Variable Overheads	7,000	
Total Variable Cost		64,725
Contribution		47,275
Less Fixed Overheads		22,000
Profit		25,275

(b) Three main benefits:

1) Management must set objectives for the business.

2) It ensures that management consider the best way of using the firm's limited resources.

3) Staff become part of the decision making process.

Answer 114 - Material Usage Variances

(a) [1,000 kg. - 1,200 kg.] x 30p

   = [200 kg.] x 30p

   = £60 adverse

(b) 3,000 bricks - 2,700 bricks x 40p

   = 300 bricks x 40p

   = £120 favourable

(c) [8,000 litres - 9,000 litres] x 46p

   = [1,000 litres] x 46p

   = £460 adverse

(d) [5,000 ounces - 5,500 ounces] x 80p

   = [500 ounces] x 80p

   = £400 adverse

(e) 2,000 pints - 1,700 pints x 32p

   = 300 pints x 32p

   = £96 favourable

(f) 20 lengths - 18 lengths x £80

   = 2 lengths x £80

   = £160 favourable

Answer 115 - Direct Labour Variances

(a)	51 - 30	£21 Favourable
(b)	3 - 3	-
(c)	50 - 99	49 Adverse
(d)	8 - 4	4 Adverse
(e)	8 - 16	8 Adverse
(f)	14 - 10.5	3.5 Favourable

Answer 116 - Material Price Variances

(a)	1,200 x .03	36 Adverse
(b)	2,700 x .02	54 Favourable
(c)	9,000 x .01	90 Adverse
(d)	5,500 x .03	165 Adverse
(e)	1,700 X .01	17 Favourable
(f)	18 x £5	90 Favourable

Answer 117 - Executive Traveller

Profit and Loss Account Budgeted Actual

	£	£
Sales	1,125,000	950,000
Less:		
Materials	500,000	450,000
Labour	250,000	300,000
Variable Overheads	175,000	175,000
Fixed Overheads	100,000	112,500
	1,025,000	1,037,500
Profit/(Loss)	100,000	(87,500)
Budgeted Profit		£100,000
Sales Variance Adverse	(£175,000)	
Materials Favourable	£50,000	
Labour Adverse	(£50,000)	
Fixed O'hd Var. Adverse	(£12,500)	
		187,500
Actual Loss		(£87,500)

Answer 118 - The Kitchen Mouldings Company

Profit and Loss Account Budgeted Actual

	£	£
Sales	150,000	130,000
Less:		
Materials	45,000	48,500
Labour	30,000	27,000
Variable Overheads	15,000	15,000
Fixed Overheads	15,000	14,000
	105,000	104,500
Profit	45,000	25,500
Budgeted Profit		£45,000
Sales Variance Adverse	(£20,000)	
Materials Adverse	£3,500)	
Labour Favourable	£3,000	
Fixed O'hd Var. Favourable	£1,000	
		(19,500)
Actual Profit		£25,500

Answer 119 - Irons and Woods

Budgeted Profit and Loss Account

	£	£
Sales (30,000 units at £45 per unit)		450,000
Less Variable Costs		
Materials	240,000	
Labour	120,000	
Total Variable Cost		360,000
Contribution		90,000
Less Fixed Costs		60,000
Profit		30,000

Material Variance:

	£	
Standard Price of Materials		
£24 per unit x 27,000 units	216,000	
Actual Cost	204,000	
	12,000	F

Labour Rate Variance:

	£	
Standard Wage Rate	108,000	
Actual wage Rate	123,000	
	15,000	A

Factory Overhead:

	£	
Standard Overhead	54,000	
Actual Overhead	48,000	
	6,000	F

	£
Budgeted Profit	30,000

Variance	Adverse £	Favourable £	
Materials		12,000	
Labour	15,000		
Overheads		6,000	
	15,000	18,000	3,000 F

Actual Net Profit £33,000

189

Answer 120 - The Welsh Honey Farm

RECEIPTS	Jan £	Feb £	Mar £	Apl £	May £	June £
Sales	65,000	73,000	120,000	140,000	110,000	130,000

PAYMENTS

Var. Costs	33,000	40,000	70,000	85,000	65,000	80,000
Fixed Costs	15,000	15,000	20,000	20,000	20,000	20,000
Taxation		8,000		22,000		
Dividends			35,000			
Total	48,000	63,000	125,000	105,000	107,000	100,000

BALANCE

Op. Bal.	15,000	32,000	42,000	37,000	72,000	75,000
Receipts	65,000	73,000	120,000	140,000	110,000	130,000
Payments	48,000	63,000	125,000	105,000	107,000	100,000
Cl. Bal	32,000	42,000	37,000	72,000	75,000	105,000

Note: In this case receipts is total sales but if there were any other inflows such as an issue of shares, or sale of fixed assets then these other items would be included in the total receipts.

Answer 121 - The Woollen Rug Company

RECEIPTS	Jan	Feb	Mar	Apl	May	June
	£	£	£	£	£	£
Sales	37,200	39,000	48,000	39,200	40,800	52,000

PAYMENTS

Raw. Mat.	16,740	17,550	21,600	17,640	15,120	14,166
Lab. Costs.	7,440	7,800	9,600	7,840	6,720	6,296
Var. O'hd.	2,790	2,925	3,600	2,940	2,520	2,361
Fixed O'hd	9,000	9,000	9,000	9,000	9,000	9,000
Machinery		15,000		8,000		
Leasing	800	800	800	800	800	800
Taxation			33,000			
Total	36,770	53,075	77,600	46,270	34,160	32,623

BALANCE

Op. Bal.	(47,859)	(47,429)	(61,504)	(91,104)	(98,124)	(91,484)
Receipts	37,200	39,000	48,000	39,200	40,800	52,000
Payments	36,770	53,075	77,600	46,220	34,160	32,623
Cl. Bal.	(47,429)	(61,504)	(91,104)	(98,124)	(91,484)	(72,107)

Note: This company is overdrawn and therefore, has a negative cash position. Until the company has a positive cash flow any receipts merely reduce the deficit and so payments increase it again.

Answer 122 - Leather Boots Ltd.

RECEIPTS	Jan	Feb	Mar	Apl	May	June
Sales	£	£	£	£	£	£
Cash	29,250	17,550	19,500	18,525	12,675	10,725
Credit	102,375	87,750	52,650	58,500	55,575	38,025
Total	131,625	105,300	72,150	77,025	68,250	48,750

PAYMENTS	Jan	Feb	Mar	Apl	May	June
Raw Mat	40,800	25,200	28,800	21,000	18,000	16,800
Dir. Lab.	20,400	12,600	14,400	10,540	9,000	8,400
Var. O'hd.	8,000	8,000	8,000	8,000	8,000	8,000
Leasing.	2,000	2,000	2,000	2,000	2,000	2,000
Rent	8,000	8,000	8,000	8,000	8,000	8,000
Total	79,200	55,000	61,200	49,500	45,000	43,200

BALANCE	Jan	Feb	Mar	Apl	May	June
Op. Bal	60,000	112,425	161,925	172,875	200,400	223,650
Receipts	131,625	105,300	72,150	77,025	68,250	48,750
Payments	79,200	55,800	61,200	49,500	45,000	43,200
Cl. Bal.	112,425	161,925	172,875	200,400	223,650	229,200

Answer 123 - The Griffin Paint Company

RECEIPTS	Jan	Feb	Mar	Apl	May	June
Sales	£	£	£	£	£	£
Cash	11,280	14,100	7,520	8,930	6,580	7,520
Credit	37,600	45,120	56,400	30,080	35,720	26,320
Total	48,880	59,220	63,920	39,010	42,300	33,840

PAYMENTS

Fixed Costs	15,000	15,000	15,000	15,000	15,000	15,000
Raw Mat	20,000	24,000	28,000	28,000	22,000	25,000
Dir. Lab	7,000	7,000	5,500	6,250	4,500	4,250
Var. O'hd.	700	700	550	625	450	425
	1,800	2,100	2,100	1,650	1,875	1,350
Leasing	800	800	800	800	800	800
Loan Rep.					10,000	
Total	45,300	49,600	51,950	52,325	54,625	46,825

BALANCE

Op. Bal	80,000	83,580	93,200	105,170	91,855	79,530
Receipts	48,880	59,220	63,920	39,010	42,300	33,840
Payments	45,300	49,600	51,950	52,325	54,625	46,825
Cl. Bal.	83,580	93,200	105,170	91,855	79,530	66,545

Answer 124

(a) source;	(b) application;	(c) application;	(d) application;
(e) application;	(f) source;	(g) source;	(h) source;
(i) application;	(j) application;	(k) application;	(l) source;
(m) source;	(n) application;	(o) source;	(p) source;

Answer 125

(a) source;	(b) source;	(c) source;	(d) source;
(e) application;	(f) application;	(g) application;	(h) application;
(i) application;	(j) source;	(k) source;	(l) application;

Answer 126   need to paste correct answer.

(a) source;	(b) source;	(c) source;	(d) source;
(e) application;	(f) application;	(g) application;	(h) application;
(i) application;	(j) source;	(k) source;	(l) application;
(m) source;	(n) source;		

Answer 127 - The Ross Garden Nursery

Cash Flow Statement for Year Ended 31 December Year 7

		£
Cash flow from operating activities		12,000
Investing Activities		
Payments to acquire tangible fixed assets		(12,000)

		NIL

		£
Reconciliation of Operating Profit		
To Net Cash Flow Investment From		
Operating Activities		
Operating Profit		32,000
Depreciation		-
Increase in Stocks		(20,000)
Increase in Debtors		(15,000)
Increase in Creditors		15,000

Net Cash Flow From Operating Activities		12,000

	Yr. 7	Yr. 6	Change in Yr.
	£	£	£
Increase in Cash and			
Cash Equivalents			
Cash at Bank and in Hand	17,000	7,000	10,000
Short Term Loan	(10,000)	-	(10,000)
	------	-----	------
	7,000	7,000	Nil
	------	-----	------

195

Answer 128 - The Patisserie

Cash Flow Statement for Year Ended 31 December Year 4

	£
Cash flow from operating activities	7,000
Investing Activities	
Payments to acquire tangible fixed assets	(27,000)
	20,000

FINANCING:	£	
Issue of Ord. Shares	10,000	
Long Term Loans	15,000	
		25,000
Increase in cash		5,000

Reconciliation of Operating Profit
To Net Cash Flow Investment From
Operating Activities

	£
Operating Profit	28,000
Increase in Stock	(12,000)
Increase in Debtors	(10,000)
Increase in Creditors	1,000
Net Cash Flow From Operating Activities	7,000

	Yr. 4 £	Yr. 3 £	Change in Yr. £
Increase in Cash and Cash Equivalents			
Cash at Bank and in Hand	13,000	8,000	5,000

Answer 129 - The Whole Wheat Bakery

a) Working capital is the short term money used to finance a business. A firm's working capital can be calculated by subtracting its current liabilities from its current assets

b) In the short term a firm's profit and cash are not the same because a sale is recorded when it is made and not when the cash is received - the realisation concept.

c) Reduce stocks and set minimum and maximum stock levels. Improve debtor collection times, increase the time taken to pay creditors, prepare cash budgets and monitor the working capital cycle.

Answer 130 - Acquarians

Ratio	Last Year	This Year
Raw Materials ------------------- Raw Materials Used	22,000 x 365 ------------------- 65,000	79,000 x 365 ------------------- 165,000
DAYS	124 days	174 days
Work in Progress ------------------- Cost of Goods Made	14,600 x 365 ------------------- 133,000	47,450 x 365 ------------------- 172,500
DAYS	161 days	239 days
Finished Goods Stock ------------------- Cost of Goods Sold	22,000 x 365 ------------------- 74,000	48,000 x 365 ------------------- 179,000
DAYS	109 days	98 days
Debtors Collection ------------------- Sales	14,300 x 365 ------------------- 130,000	42,000 x 365 ------------------- 240,000
DAYS	20 days	32 days
Creditors Payment ------------------- Purchases	8,240 x 365 ------------------- 58,000	37,500 x 365 ------------------- 93,340
DAYS	(52)	(68)
Cash Operating Cycle	362 days	475 days

Note: Credit received reduces the cash operating cycle and is therefore deducted.

Answer 131 - Barton Lodge Crafts

Ratio	Last Year	This Year
Raw Materials	300,000 x 365	450,000 x 365
Raw Materials Used	190,00	240,000
DAYS	58 days	68 days
Work in Progress	45,000 x 365	60,000 x 365
Cost of Goods Made	390,000	525,000
DAYS	42 days	42 days
Finished Goods Stock	30,000 x 365	75, x 365
Cost of Goods Sold	370,000	490,000
DAYS	30 days	56 days
Debtors Collection	80,000 x 365	120,000 x 365
Sales	500,000	650,000
DAYS	58 days	67 days
Creditors Payment	60,000 x 365	95,000 x 365
Purchases	45,000	60,000
DAYS	(49) days	(55) days
Cash Operating Cycle	139 days	178 days

Answer 132

a) Acid Test - Current Assets Less Stock/Current Liabilities - Measures a firm's liquidity.

b) Primary Ratio - Profit x 100/Capital Employed - Calculates the return on capital employed.

c) Gearing - Debt/Equity - Measures ratio of borrowed capital to share capital.

d) Interest Cover - Profit before Interest and Tax/Interest Paid Calculates the number of times a firm can meet its interest charges out of profits.

e) Current Ratio - Current Assets/Current Liabilities - measures a firm's liquidity.

f) Divided Yield - Ordinary Dividend per Share x 100/Market Price per Share - It calculates the real return a shareholder receives when a dividend is paid by taking into account the market price of the share and not the shares nominal value.

g) Earnings Per Share - Profit after Tax and Preference Share Dividend/Number of Issued Ordinary Shares - Calculates the return a company can earn with its share capital.

h) Stock Turnover - Stock/Cost of Goods x 365 - Calculates the number of times stock is sold during a financial year.

i) Debtors Collection Period - Debtors x 365/Sales - Calculates the time taken to collect debts.

j) Price to Earnings - Present Market Price Per Ordinary Share/Annual Earnings Per Share - It calculates the number of years it would take for the firm's earnings to equal the current share price.

Answer 133 - The Diverse Engineering Group

a)   The additional debt will increase interest payments. If sales and profits fall the increased debt may have an adverse effect on cash flow. If a company cannot meet its interest payments it may be forced into liquidation. Increased debt capital will increase the firm's gearing ratio which could adversely affect the share price and reduce its credit rating thereby increasing the cost of any future borrowings.

b)   If a firm is unable to meet its interest payments or repay the sum borrowed it may need to restructure its debts. This can take the form of either lengthening the time period of the loan or the lender agreeing to turn current interest payments into additional debt. Sometimes the lender may seek both of these options.

c)   A highly geared company is a more risky investment particularly if sales and profits fall. So long as the firm is profitable it should in theory be able to pay higher dividends than a lowly geared company because it has fewer shareholders. If the company can increase its profits and solve its current problems it should be able to increase its dividend payments thereby leading to an increase in its share price.

Answer 134 - Transic plc

Increase in turnover (sales) of 21%. Trading profits have increased by 14%. There has been an increase in interest payments. This may be because interest rates are now higher than last year but it is more likely that the company has increased its borrowing. Interest charges have risen by 63%.

The company is able to increase the amount of profit available for distribution as dividend and has increased its earnings per share. Unfortunately retained profits which will be used to finance new investment has fallen slightly. Nevertheless a share holder would be pleased with these results particularly from a company operating in a recession.

Answer 135 - The Takeover Battle

a) Overseas Visitor

b) The higher the gearing the greater the risk to an equity investor and therefore shares in Overseas Visitor would be the riskier investment assuming all other factors to be equal.

c) It has fewer shareholders and therefore, there are less people to share the total sum available for distribution as dividend.

d) Depends upon investors attitude to risk but Overseas Visitor is currently producing much better financial returns for investors.

Answer 136 - Harlequin Tours

a) It would increase the firm's gearing. If an additional £300,000 of borrowed capital was raised the gearing ratio would rise to 1:1 thereby making the company highly geared.

b) Increased Gearing. May well make it difficult to raise additional debt capital. May depress share price. Increased investor risk.

c) Company may be reluctant to increase share capital either by having a rights issue or issuing new shares because it will dilute earnings. Also shareholders may be reluctant to invest more because of low share price or poor dividend payments. Also interest rates may be low relative to the cost of equity finance thereby making debt capital more attractive.

Answer 137 - The Wine Grotto

a) Current Ratio = 2:1
b) Acid Test = 1.7:1
c) Stock Turnover = 132 days
d) Debtors Ratio = 95 days
e) Return on Capital Employed = 23%
Note: Please see appendix for complete list of ratios.

Answer 138

Project TYA 2 Years; Project TYB 2 Years; Project TYC 3 Years

Answer 139

Project XZ1: 2 Years and 7 Months
Project XZ1: 3 Years and 8 Months
Project XZ3: 3 Years and 6 Months
Note: Pay back time calculated to nearest whole number.

Answer 140

			£
Formula:	Average Profit	Total Inflows	67,500
	-----------------------	Less Investment	30,000
	Average Investment		--------------
			37,500

Average Profit £37,500/5 = £7,500

$$\frac{\text{Average Profit}}{\text{Average Investment}} \quad \frac{£7,500}{£15,000} \times 100 = 50\%$$

Note: Average profit is calculated by adding up total inflows and then subtracting the initial investment thereby calculating the total profit. If the total profit figure is divided by the number of years the average profit can be calculated.

Answer 141

$$\frac{\text{Average Profit}}{\text{Average Investment}} \quad \frac{£38,300}{£40,000} \times 100 = 96\%$$

202

Answer 142

Year Cash	Inflow Net £	D/F 16%	Net Present Value £
1	33,540	0.862	28,911
2	47,840	0.743	35,545
3	66,300	0.641	42,498
4	92,479	0.552	51,048
5	102,580	0.476	48,828
6	126,389	0.410	51,819
7	167,394	0.354	59,257
Net Present Value			317,906

Note: D/F = Discount Factor

Answer 143

Capital £	5% £	7% £	10% £	12% £	15% £
10,000					
Ten Years	16,290	19,670	25,940	31,060	40,460

Answer 144

	8% £	6% £	10% £	12% £	4% £	16% £
Capital	17,000	20,000	33,500	45,700	90,000	66,000
Ten Years	36,703	35,820	86,899	141,944	133,200	291,126

Answer 145

Year	Cash Inflow £	D/F 12%	Net Present Value £
1	5,000	0.893	4,465
2	14,300	0.797	11,397
3	18,900	0.712	13,457
4	26,700	0.636	16,981
5	34,700	0.567	19,675
6	44,590	0.507	22,607
7	63,820	0.452	28,847

Answer 146 - Steel Stockholders Limited

Year	Investment	Cash Inflow	Cash Outflow	Net Cash Flow
	£	£	£	£
0	(250,000)	-	-	-
1		65,000	33,000	32,000
2		79,000	22,000	57,000
3		94,000	11,500	82,500
4		125,000		125,000
5		146,000		146,000
6		157,000		157,000

Answer 147 - Wood Supplies

Year	Investment	Cash Inflow	Cash Outflow	Net Cash Flow
	£	£	£	£
0	(180,000)	-	-	-
1		25,000	7,000	18,000
2		49,000	8,000	41,000
3		66,000	15,000	51,000
4		75,000	15,000	60,000
5		83,000	10,000	73,000
6		85,000	-	85,000
7		90,000	-	90,000

pa.

Answer 148 - The Village Lawn Tennis Club

Year	Investment £	D/F 8%	Net Cash Flow £	N.P.V. £
0	14,000	-	-	(14,000)
1		0.926	9,100	8,427
2		0.857	4,750	4,071
3		0.794	9,300	7,384
4		0.735	11,950	8,783
5		0.681	22,500	15,322
6		0.630	25,000	15,750

Net Present Value 45,737

Answer 149 - Mountain Tours

(a) Pay back:

	£	£
Initial Investment		120,000
Year One	35,000	
Year Two	57,000	92,000
	----------	----------
Shortfall		28,000

Year 3 Inflows £65,000/12 months = £5,333 inflow per month

$$\frac{\text{Shortfall}}{\text{Monthly Inflow}} = \frac{£28,000}{£5,333} = 5 \text{ months}$$

Pay Back Time 2 Years 5 Months

(b) Accounting Rate of Return

$$\frac{\text{Average Profit}}{\text{Average Investment}} = \frac{£63,000}{£60,000} \times 100 = 105\%$$

(c) Net Present Value

Year	Investment £	Cash Inflow £	D/F 14%	N.P.V £
0	(120,000)	-	-	(120,000)
1		35,000	0.877	30,695
2		57,000	0.769	43,833
3		64,000	0.675	43,200
4		70,000	0.592	41,440
5		89,000	0.519	46,191
Net Present Value				85,359

Answer 150 - Travel Tours

(a) Pay back:

	£	£
Initial Investment		65,000
Year One	26,000	
Year Two	33,000	
	------------	59,000
Shortfall		------------
		6,000

Year 3 £36,000/12 = £3,000 per month

	£	
Shortfall	6,000	
--------------------	----------	= 2 months
Monthly Inflow	3,000	

Payback time 2 Years 2 Months

(b) Accounting Rate of Return:

Average Profit	£31,333	
------------------------	-----------	x 100 = 96%
Average Investment	£32,500	

(c) Net Present Value:

Year	Investment £	Cash Inflow £	D/F 10%	N.P.V £
0	(65,000)	-	-	(65,000)
1		26,000	0.909	23,634
2		33,000	0.826	27,258
3		36,000	0.751	27,036
4		45,000	0.683	30,735
5		48,000	0.621	29,808
Net Present Value				73,471

Glossary of Financial Terms

Absorbed Cost Costs which have been spread over operational units, e.g. job, batch unit or contract.

Accounting The system of recording accounting information using double entry book-keeping.

Accounting Equation The assets of a firm are equal to its liabilities. Assets are things which the firm owns, even if it has not yet paid for them, and liabilities are claims against the firm.

Accounting Period The amount of time covered by the financial statements of a business.

Accounting Policies The specific accounting bases chosen and followed by a firm which the management believe are the most appropriate and which will present its results and financial position fairly.

Accounts Receivable: A firm's credit sales to customers.

Accrual An amount owing at the time the annual accounts are prepared. The sum owing will be shown in the balance sheet under current liabilities.

Acid Test Ratio Current assets less stock/Current liabilities. This ratio shows the firm's ability to meet its short term liabilities out of its cash and near cash assets, such as debtors.

Accrued Expenses Expenses which are recognised when goods received or services provided during a given accounting period have not been invoiced, or when wages have been earned but not paid by the end of that period.

Annual Accounts The set of accounts comprising a balance sheet together with a profit and loss account and a statement of source and application of funds together with directors' report and other information as required by Companies' Act 1985. (See chapter on Company Accounts)

Appropriation Account A financial statement which shows how the firm's net profit after taxation has been used.

Apportioned Cost Costs which have been spread over cost centres.

Assets Everything of value owned by a business.

Authorisd Share Capital This is the amount of money which the company took power to raise when it was formed.

207

Avoidable Cost	A cost not incurred if an action is not taken, or is discontinued.
Bad Debt	A debt which has not been paid. It is an expense to the firm and the amount will be shown in the profit and loss account.
Balance Sheet	A statement showing the assets and liabilities of a business at a particular date.
Basis	The cash price less the futures price.
Basis Point	The smallest increment for measuring price.
Bear	A person who believes that a share price will fall.
Bid Price	The price a buyer will pay for a financial security or futures contract.
Bond	A financial security (certificate) showing the indebtedness of an organisation, together with the rate of interest payable and the date, if applicable, when it will be repaid.
Bonus Issue	The issuing of shares to existing shareholders by distributing a company's reserves as shares. No monetary payments are made. Sometimes called a scrip issue.
Book Value	The historical cost of an asset, less depreciation accumulated over the asset's life.
Break Even	The amount of sales needed to cover a firm's fixed and variable costs. Above the break-even point the firm makes a profit and below it makes a loss.
Bull	A person who believes share prices will rise.
Called Up Capital	This refers to shares issued by the company but not yet fully paid for by the shareholders.
Capital	The long term money which is financing a business.
Capital Employed	The long term capital which finances a firm. It includes share capital, reserves and loan capital (debentures, secured loan stock and unsecured loan stock).
Capital Expenditure	Money spent by the company on purchasing fixed assets.
Capital Loss	Losses made on the sale of fixed assets.
Capital Profit	Money made on the sale of fixed assets.

208

Capital Receipts	Money received by a company on the issue of shares and debentures.
Capital Reserve	Reserves which are not available for distribution as dividends, e.g., any surplus arising as a premium on the issue of shares or debentures.
Carriage Inwards	The cost of having goods delivered. It increases the cost of purchases and the amount paid is shown in the trading account.
Carriage Outwards	The cost of delivering goods to customers. The amount is treated as an expense and is shown in the profit and loss account.
Cash Budget	Budget drawn up to enable the firm to forecast future cash receipts and payments.
Cash Flow	Accounting term used to describe the cash generated and used during a given financial period.
Cash Operating Cycle	Length of time a firm has to wait before it receives cash.
Contingent Liability	Obligation which may arise in respect of past events. such as the outcome of a law case.
Convertible Loan Stock	A loan which gives the holder the right to convert to other securities, normally ordinary shares, at a pre-determined rate and time.
Corporation Tax	Tax calculated on a company's profits.
Cost Centre	A location, individual,or item of equipment for which costs may be ascertained and used for purposes of control or product costing.
Cost Unit	Item of product (usually of output or service) to which costs can be allocated or attributed.
Cumulative Preference Shares	These shares allow the owners to receive arrears of dividend before dividends are paid to the ordinary shareholders.
Current Assets	These are assets of a circulating nature which are acquired by a business in order to trade with other companies or individuals. They are shown in the balance sheet in order of liquidity, with the least liquid shown first. The order is stock, debtors,(people who owe the firm money) bank and cash balances.
Current Worth	See Net Worth.
Debenture	Normally a secured loan over the assets of a company. The debenture holders do not own the company but they are entitled to interest payments. If the interest is not paid, the debenture holders can sell the firm's assets so that they can recover their money.

Deferred Taxation	An amount provided to equalise the timing differences which arise between the tax charge based on the pre- tax profit in the profit and loss account and the actual tax liability, as separately computed in accordance with tax legislation. Transfers are made to a deferred taxation account, the balance on which is shown separately in the balance sheet.
Depreciation	Most assets wear out as they are used. Machinery wears out and buildings deteriorate. An allowance, called depreciation, for this fall in value must be included in the firm's accounts.
Direct Cost	A cost which can be associated wholly and specifically with a cost unit, e.g., machine, department or individual.
Discount Allowed	The cost of allowing a debtor to pay a smaller sum than the original bill if the debt is settled early. The cost is shown as an expense in the profit and loss account.
Discount Received	Money given off a bill for settling it early. It is treated as income and added to gross profit.
Discretionary Cost	A programmed cost which is subject to management discretion and control.
Dividend	A distribution to shareholders out of profits, usually in the form of cash.
Equity	The share capital of the business plus reserves.
Factoring	The technical term used to describe selling credit sales (debtors) to a factoring house or bank for cash.
Fixed Assets	Assets acquired for retention in a business for the purpose of providing goods or services. Fixed assets are not held for resale in the normal course of business. Examples are Land and Buildings, Plant and Machinery.
Fixed Cost	A cost unaffected by change of activity level in a given period of time.
Gearing	The ratio of a firm's debt to equity capital. In the U.S.A. it is called leverage.
Goodwill	Sum of money paid for the goods of a business. When a business is purchased any amount paid in excess of its net assets (Total Assets less Liabilities) represents the value placed on goodwill.
Gross Profit	The profit made on goods and services sold before expenses are deducted. The percentage profit can be calculated by the following formula:

$$\frac{\text{Profit} \times 100}{\text{Cost Price}}$$

Historical Cost	The original cost of acquiring the fixed asset.
Incremental Cost	Additional cost of one course of action over another.
Indirect Cost	A cost which cannot be directly allocated but can be apportioned to cost centres and cost units, e.g., overhead costs.
Intangible Asset	Assets which do not have a physical identity, e.g., goodwill.
Issued Share Capital	The number of shares which have been issued to shareholders and which have been fully paid for.
Leverage	See gearing
Liquid Asset	Cash and any other financial security which can be converted quickly into cash.
Listed Investment	An investment which is quoted on a recognised stock exchange, e.g., London, Tokyo, New York.
Marginal Cost	The amount of cost incurred at a given level of output by increasing the volume of output by one.
Minority Interest	Shares held in a subsidiary company by shareholders other than a holding company or its nominees.
Net Profit	The gross profit less expenses.
Net Worth	A concept denoting the excess of the book values of all assets over liabilities. In a company it represents the interests of shareholders, i.e. the paid-up share capital and reserves. If the assets are taken at current values, instead of book values, the concept is known as current worth.
Nominal Value	The face value of a share or loan stock.
Off Balance Sheet Finance	A source of finance not shown on the balance sheet because there is no corresponding asset, e.g., an operating lease.
Ordinary Shareholders	These are the owners of the company. They are entitled to a dividend, which is a share of the firm's profit.
Paid Up Capital	This refers to shares which have been issued by the company and which have been fully paid for by the shareholders.
Pay Back	The time taken for inflows from an investment to equal its cost.
Preference Shareholders	Owners of these shares enjoy preferential rights over the ordinary shareholders. Their dividend is normally at a pre-determined rate and they

receive it before the ordinary shareholders are paid. The Articles of Association sometimes make special provision for the preference shareholders by allowing them to be repaid in full before before the ordinary shareholders, in the event of the company being wound up. If there is no such provision, then all shareholders share equally the remaining assets of the company.

Prime Cost   Total of direct material, direct labour and direct expenses.

Provisions   Amounts written off or retained, by way of providing for depreciation, renewals or diminution of assets, or retained to provide for a known liability, the extent of which cannot be expressly determined, e.g., provision for bad debts.

Relevant Cost   Those costs which are pertinent to the decision being made.

Reserves   These are unappropriated profits (not distributed to shareholders as dividends) or, surplus funds made possible by the revaluation of fixed assets or, the issue of shares for more than their nominal value.

Retained Profits   These consist of undistributed profits and can be used to pay dividends, maintain the business, or absorb losses. The revenue reserve is made up of the general reserve and the profit and loss account, as shown in the balance sheet.

Returns Inwards   Sales returned to the firm by customers. The amount reduces sales and is shown in the trading account. Sometimes referred to as net sales.

Returns Outwards   Purchases returned by the firm to suppliers. The amount reduces purchases and is shown in the trading account. Sometimes referred to as net purchases.

Rights Issue   The raising of new capital by inviting existing shareholders to subscribe for shares on preferential terms. The shares can generally be bought for less than their stock market price.

Secured Creditors   Creditors whose claims are wholly or partly secured on the assets of the business.

Share Premium   This shows that the shares were once sold for more than their nominal value; the surplus is shown in the balance sheet as a capital reserve.

Sinking Fund   A fund created for the redemption of a liability. The aim is to set aside a certain sum which will, at a set date in the future, be sufficient to meet a liability.

Source and   A financial statement which shows the external and internal sources from
Application of   which funds have been obtained to finance a business during a given
Funds Statement   accounting period, and the manner in which the funds have been deployed.

212

Standard Cost	A predetermined cost, calculated on the basis of a desired level of operating efficiency and activity level.
Stocks	Raw materials, work in progress, finished goods and goods in transit, or on consignment, at the end of an accounting period.
Sunk Cost	Those costs invested in a project which will not be recovered, even if the project is discontinued.
Tangible Assets	Assets having a physical identity, e.g., land and buildings, plant and machinery.
Trading Account	A financial statement which shows the revenue from sales, the cost of those sales and the gross profit arising during a given accounting period.
Unappropriated Profits	Profits which the company has reinvested in the firm, instead of distributing them as dividends to the shareholders.
Unlisted Investment	An investment which is not quoted on a recognised stock exchange.
Unsecured Loan	Loan stock which carries interest, but is not secured on any of the assets of the company.
Variable Cost	Costs which vary directly with the level of activity (output), e.g., direct labour and direct materials.
Variance	A difference between the standard cost and the actual cost. The variance may be adverse, in which case the actual cost was more than the standard cost, or favourable, in which case it was less. In either case the reason for the variance must be analysed by management.
Working Capital	The difference between a firm's current assets and its current liabilities.
Work in Progress	Materials, components or products in various stages of completion during a manufacturing process. The term also applies to partly completed contracts.

The Key Accounting Ratios

RATIO	CALCULATION

Ratios Which Assess Liquidity

Current Ratio	$\dfrac{\text{Current Assets}}{\text{Current Liabilities}}$
Acid Test Ratio	$\dfrac{\text{Current Assets Less Stock}}{\text{Current Liabilities}}$
Sales to Working Capital	$\dfrac{\text{Sales}}{\text{Working Capital}}$
Sales to Capital Employed	$\dfrac{\text{Sales}}{\text{Capital Employed}}$
Net Working Capital to Sales	$\dfrac{\text{Stock + Debtors - Creditors}}{\text{Sales}}$

Ratios Which Assess Profitability

Primary Ratio or Return on Capital Employed	$\dfrac{\text{Profit} \times 100}{\text{Capital Employed}}$
Gross Profit To Sales	$\dfrac{\text{Gross Profit} \times 100}{\text{Sales}}$
Net Profit To Sales	$\dfrac{\text{Net Profit} \times 100}{\text{Sales}}$

214

Ratios Which Assess How Effectively A Firm Uses Its Assets

Stock Turnover

$$\frac{\text{Cost of Goods Sold} \times 365}{\text{Average Stock}}$$

Debtors Collection Period

$$\frac{\text{Debtors} \times 365}{\text{Sales}}$$

Time Taken To Pay Creditors

$$\frac{\text{Creditors} \times 365}{\text{Purchases}}$$

Sales To Fixed Assets

$$\frac{\text{Sales}}{\text{Fixed Assets}}$$

Fixed Assets To Current Assets

$$\frac{\text{Fixed Assets}}{\text{Current Assets}}$$

Ratios Which Assess A Firm's Capital Structure

Gearing ratio

$$\frac{\text{Debt}}{\text{Equity (Share Capital)}}$$

Shareholders' Investment

$$\frac{\text{Shareholders Investment}}{\text{Total Assets}}$$

Interest Cover

$$\frac{\text{Profit Before Interest and Tax}}{\text{Interest Paid}}$$

Ratios Which Assess The Returns Paid To Investors

Earning Per Share

$$\frac{\text{Profit After Tax and Preference Share Dividend}}{\text{Number of Issued Ordinary Shares}}$$

Dividend Yield

$$\frac{\text{Ordinary Dividend Per Share} \times 100}{\text{Market Price per Share}}$$

Dividend Cover	Profit After Tax less Preference Dividend
	Gross Dividend on Ordinary Shares

Price Earnings	Present Market Price Per Ordinary Share
	Annual Earnings Per Share

Key Variances

Variance	Formula
Material Price	Expected Price of Material Used Less Actual Price of Material Used
Material Usage	(Expected Quantity of Material Used Less Actual Quantity of Material Used) Multiplied by Standard Price.
Labour Rate	Expected Cost of Hours Worked Less Actual Cost
Variable Overhead Expenditure	Expected Cost of Hours Worked Less Actual Cost
Variable Overhead Efficiency	(Expected Hours Worked Less Actual Hours Worked) Multiplied by Standard Rate
Fixed Overhead Volume	Budgeted Fixed Overheads Less Expected Fixed Overheads for the Actual Production.
Sales Price	Expected Revenue From Units Sold Less Actual Revenue
Sales Volume	(Expected Sales (units) Less Actual Sales) Multiplied by Standard Profit/Unit

216

DCF TABLES

Compound Sum of £1 (CVIF) $S = P(1 + r)^N$

Period	1%	2%	3%	4%	5%	6%	7%
1	1.010	1.020	1.030	1.040	1.050	1.060	1.070
2	1.020	1.040	1.061	1.082	1.102	1.124	1.145
3	1.030	1.061	1.093	1.125	1.158	1.191	1.225
4	1.041	1.082	1.126	1.170	1.216	1.262	1.311
5	1.051	1.104	1.159	1.217	1.276	1.338	1.403
6	1.062	1.126	1.194	1.265	1.340	1.419	1.501
7	1.072	1.149	1.230	1.316	1.407	1.504	1.606
8	1.083	1.172	1.267	1.369	1.477	1.594	1.718
9	1.094	1.195	1.305	1.423	1.551	1.689	1.838
10	1.105	1.219	1.344	1.480	1.629	1.791	1.967
11	1.116	1.243	1.384	1.539	1.710	1.898	2.105
12	1.127	1.268	1.426	1.601	1.796	2.012	2.252
13	1.138	1.294	1.469	1.665	1.886	2.133	2.410
14	1.149	1.319	1.513	1.732	1.980	2.261	2.579
15	1.161	1.346	1.558	1.801	2.079	2.397	2.759
16	1.173	1.373	1.605	1.873	2.183	2.540	2.952
17	1.184	1.400	1.653	1.948	2.292	2.693	3.159
18	1.196	1.428	1.702	2.026	2.407	2.854	3.380
19	1.208	1.457	1.754	2.107	2.527	3.026	3.617
20	1.220	1.486	1.806	2.191	2.653	3.207	3.870
25	1.282	1.641	2.094	2.666	3.386	4.292	5.427
30	1.348	1.811	2.427	3.243	4.322	5.743	7.612

Period	8%	9%	10%	12%	14%	15%	16%
1	1.080	1.090	1.100	1.120	1.140	1.150	1.160
2	1.166	1.186	1.210	1.254	1.300	1.322	1.346
3	1.260	1.295	1.331	1.405	1.482	1.521	1.561
4	1.360	1.412	1.464	1.574	1.689	1.749	1.811
5	1.469	1.539	1.611	1.762	1.925	2.011	2.100
6	1.587	1.677	1.772	1.974	2.195	2.313	2.436
7	1.714	1.828	1.949	2.211	2.502	2.660	2.826
8	1.851	1.993	2.144	2.476	2.853	3.059	3.278
9	1.999	2.172	2.358	2.773	3.252	3.518	3.803
10	2.159	2.367	2.594	3.106	3.707	4.046	4.411
11	2.332	2.580	2.853	3.479	4.226	4.652	5.117
12	2.518	2.813	3.138	3.896	4.818	5.350	5.926
13	2.720	3.066	3.452	4.363	5.492	6.153	6.886
14	2.937	3.342	3.797	4.887	6.261	7.076	7.988
15	3.172	3.642	4.177	5.474	7.138	8.137	9.266
16	3.426	3.970	4.595	6.130	8.137	9.358	10.748
17	3.700	4.328	5.054	6.866	9.276	10.761	12.468
18	3.996	4.717	5.560	7.690	10.575	12.375	14.463
19	4.316	5.142	6.116	8.613	12.056	14.232	16.777
20	4.661	5.604	6.728	9.646	13.743	16.367	19.461
25	6.848	8.623	10.835	17.000	26.462	32.919	40.874
30	10.063	13.268	17.449	29.960	50.950	66.212	85.850

217

Present Value of £1 (PVIF)P $= S(1 + r)^{-N}$

Period	1%	2%	3%	4%	5%	6%	7%	8%	9%	10%	12%	14%	15%
1	0.990	0.980	0.971	0.962	0.952	0.943	0.935	0.926	0.917	0.909	0.893	0.877	0.870
2	0.980	0.961	0.943	0.925	0.907	0.890	0.873	0.857	0.842	0.826	0.797	0.769	0.756
3	0.971	0.942	0.915	0.889	0.864	0.840	0.816	0.794	0.772	0.751	0.712	0.675	0.658
4	0.961	0.924	0.889	0.855	0.823	0.792	0.763	0.735	0.708	0.683	0.636	0.592	0.572
5	0.951	0.906	0.863	0.822	0.784	0.747	0.713	0.681	0.650	0.621	0.567	0.519	0.497
6	0.942	0.888	0.838	0.790	0.746	0.705	0.666	0.630	0.596	0.564	0.507	0.456	0.432
7	0.933	0.871	0.813	0.760	0.711	0.665	0.623	0.583	0.547	0.513	0.452	0.400	0.376
8	0.923	0.853	0.789	0.731	0.677	0.627	0.582	0.540	0.502	0.467	0.404	0.351	0.327
9	0.914	0.837	0.766	0.703	0.645	0.592	0.544	0.500	0.460	0.424	0.361	0.308	0.284
10	0.905	0.820	0.744	0.676	0.614	0.558	0.508	0.463	0.422	0.386	0.322	0.270	0.247
11	0.896	0.804	0.722	0.650	0.585	0.527	0.475	0.429	0.388	0.350	0.287	0.237	0.215
12	0.887	0.788	0.701	0.625	0.557	0.497	0.444	0.397	0.356	0.319	0.257	0.208	0.187
13	0.879	0.773	0.681	0.601	0.530	0.469	0.415	0.368	0.326	0.290	0.229	0.182	0.163
14	0.870	0.758	0.661	0.577	0.505	0.442	0.388	0.340	0.299	0.263	0.205	0.160	0.141
15	0.861	0.743	0.642	0.555	0.481	0.417	0.362	0.315	0.275	0.239	0.183	0.140	0.123
16	0.853	0.728	0.623	0.534	0.458	0.394	0.339	0.292	0.252	0.218	0.163	0.123	0.107
17	0.844	0.714	0.605	0.513	0.436	0.371	0.317	0.270	0.231	0.198	0.146	0.108	0.093
18	0.836	0.700	0.587	0.494	0.416	0.350	0.296	0.250	0.212	0.180	0.130	0.095	0.081
19	0.828	0.686	0.570	0.475	0.396	0.331	0.276	0.232	0.194	0.164	0.116	0.083	0.070
20	0.820	0.673	0.554	0.456	0.377	0.312	0.258	0.215	0.178	0.149	0.104	0.073	0.061
25	0.780	0.610	0.478	0.375	0.295	0.233	0.184	0.146	0.116	0.092	0.059	0.038	0.030
30	0.742	0.552	0.412	0.308	0.231	0.174	0.131	0.099	0.075	0.057	0.033	0.020	0.015

Present Value of £1 (PVIF)P = $S(1 + r)^{-N}$ cont.

Period	16%	18%	20%	24%	28%	32%	36%	40%	50%	60%	70%	80%	90%
1	0.862	0.847	0.833	0.806	0.781	0.758	0.735	0.714	0.667	0.625	0.588	0.556	0.526
2	0.743	0.718	0.694	0.650	0.610	0.574	0.541	0.510	0.444	0.391	0.346	0.309	0.277
3	0.641	0.609	0.579	0.524	0.477	0.435	0.398	0.364	0.296	0.244	0.204	0.171	0.146
4	0.552	0.516	0.482	0.423	0.373	0.329	0.292	0.260	0.198	0.153	0.120	0.095	0.077
5	0.476	0.437	0.402	0.341	0.291	0.250	0.215	0.186	0.132	0.095	0.070	0.053	0.040
6	0.410	0.370	0.335	0.275	0.227	0.189	0.158	0.133	0.088	0.060	0.041	0.029	0.021
7	0.354	0.314	0.279	0.222	0.178	0.143	0.116	0.095	0.059	0.037	0.024	0.016	0.011
8	0.305	0.266	0.233	0.179	0.139	0.108	0.085	0.068	0.039	0.023	0.014	0.009	0.006
9	0.263	0.226	0.194	0.144	0.108	0.082	0.063	0.048	0.026	0.015	0.008	0.005	0.003
10	0.227	0.191	0.162	0.116	0.085	0.062	0.046	0.035	0.017	0.009	0.005	0.003	0.002
11	0.195	0.162	0.135	0.094	0.066	0.047	0.034	0.025	0.012	0.006	0.003	0.002	0.001
12	0.168	0.137	0.112	0.076	0.052	0.036	0.025	0.018	0.008	0.004	0.002	0.001	0.001
13	0.145	0.116	0.093	0.061	0.040	0.027	0.018	0.013	0.005	0.002	0.001	0.001	0.000
14	0.125	0.099	0.078	0.049	0.032	0.021	0.014	0.009	0.003	0.001	0.001	0.000	0.000
15	0.108	0.084	0.065	0.040	0.025	0.016	0.010	0.006	0.002	0.001	0.000	0.000	0.000
16	0.093	0.071	0.054	0.032	0.019	0.012	0.007	0.005	0.002	0.001	0.000	0.000	
17	0.080	0.060	0.045	0.026	0.015	0.009	0.005	0.003	0.001	0.000	0.000		
18	0.069	0.051	0.038	0.021	0.012	0.007	0.004	0.002	0.001	0.000			
19	0.060	0.043	0.031	0.017	0.009	0.005	0.003	0.002	0.000	0.000			
20	0.051	0.037	0.026	0.014	0.007	0.004	0.002	0.001	0.000	0.000			
25	0.024	0.016	0.010	0.005	0.002	0.001	0.000	0.000					
30	0.012	0.007	0.004	0.002	0.001	0.000	0.000						

Prescribed formats for company accounts

Balance sheet - format 1

A. Called up share capital not paid

B. Fixed assets

I Intangible assets

1. Development costs

2. Concessions, patents, licences, trade marks and similar rights and assets.

3. Goodwill

4. Payments on account

II Tangible assets

1. Land and buildings

2. Plant and machinery

3. Fixtures, fittings, tools and equipment

4. Payments on account and assets in course of construction

III Investments

1. Shares in group companies

2. Loans to group companies

3. Shares in related companies

4. Loans to related companies

5. Other investments other than loans

6. Other loans

7. Own shares

C. Current assets

I Stocks

1. Raw materials and consumables

2. Work in progress

3. Finished goods and goods for resale

4. Payments on account

II Debtors

1. Trade debtors

2. Amounts owed by group companies

3. Amounts owed by related companies

4. Other debtors

5. Called up share capital not paid

6. Prepayments and accrued income

III Investments

1. Shares in group companies

2. Own shares

3. Other investments

IV Cash at bank and in hand

D. Prepayments and Accrued income

E. Creditors: amounts falling due within one year

1. Debenture loans

2. Bank loans and overdrafts

3. Payments received on account

4. Trade creditors

5. Bills of exchange payable

6. Amounts owed to group companies

7. Amounts owed to related companies

8. Other creditors including taxation and social security

9. Accruals and deferred income

F. Net current assets (liabilities)

G. Total assets less current liabilities

H. Creditors: amounts falling due after more than one year

1. Debenture loans

2. Bank loans and overdrafts

3. Payments received on account

4. Trade creditors

5. Bills of exchange payable

6. Amounts owed to group companies

7. Amounts owed to related companies

8. Other creditors including taxation and social security

9. Accruals and deferred income

I. Provisions for liabililties and charges

1. Pensions and similar obligations

2. Taxation, including deferred taxation

3. Other provisions

J. Accruals and deferred income

K. Capital and reserves

I Called up share capital

II Share premium account

III Revaluation reserve

IV Other reserves

1. Capital redemption reserve

2. Reserve for own shares

3. Reserves provided for by the articles of association

4. Other reserves

V Profit and loss account

Profit and loss account - formats 1 and 2

Format 1
1. Turnover
2. Cost of Sales
3. Gross profit or loss
4. Distribution costs
5. Administrative expenses
6. Other operating income
7. Income from shares in group companies
8. Income from shares in related companies
9. Income from other fixed asset investments
10. Other interest receivable and similar income
11. Amounts written off investments
12. Interest payable and similar charges
13. Tax on profit or loss on ordinary activities
14. Profit or loss on ordinary activities after taxation
15. Extraordinary income
16. Extraordinary charges
17. Extraordinary profit or loss
18. Tax on extraordinary profit or loss
19. Other taxes not shown under the above items
20. Profit or loss for the financial year

Format 2

1. Turnover
2. Change in stocks of finished goods and in work in progress
3. Own work capitalised
4. Other operating income
5. (a) Raw materials and consumables
   (b) Other external charges
6. Staff costs:
   (a) wages and salaries
   (b) social security costs
   (c) other pension costs
7. (a) Depreciation and other amounts written off tangible and intangible fixed assets
   (b) Exceptional amounts written off current assets
8. Other operating charges

9. Income from shares in group companies
10. Income from shares in related companies
11. Income from other fixed asset investments
12. Other interest receivable and similar income
13. Amounts written off investments
14. Interest payable and similar charges
15. Tax on profit or loss on ordinary activities
16. Profit or loss on ordinary activities after taxation
17. Extraordinary income
18. Extraordinary charges
19. Extraordinary profit or loss
20. Tax on extraordinary profit or loss
21. Other taxes not shown under the above items
22. Profit or loss for the financial year

PEG Series (Practical Exercises for Groups)
Editor - Humphrey Shaw

Finance & Accounting: cases and problems

150 problems and cases on financial accounting & control from first steps to medium difficulty. 150 cases and problems in financial management specially written for the person studying the subject from first steps to medium difficulty. Examples span a range of industries, including hotel & catering & leisure. With answers. Oct 1992 pre-publication £8.95 (£9.95 1/1/93) isbn 1 85450 013 9

Decision Making

40 case studies in financial and quantitative management. With common accounting ratios, prescribed formats for company accounts, glossary and DCF/NPV tables.
Book - £5.95   isbn 0 946139 42 3
Tutor's Manual (worked answers, notes, OHPs) £49.00 isbn 0 946139 47 4

Entrepreneurial Decision Making

50 case studies on small and medium-sized businesses, each with crucial decisions to make. With a Glossary and discounted cash flow tables, the book has cases on Individual, Business Environment & Enterprise, Organisational, Marketing and Financial decisions.
Book - £5.95   isbn 0 946139 69 5
Tutor's Manual (worked answers, notes, OHPs) £49.00   isbn 0 946139 74 1

Computer simulations

Football Manager
Restaurant Manager
Property Manager
Ideal for residential weekend or post-experience short courses.
£69.95+VAT for disk (3½" or 5¼") and Tutor's Manual

Diagnostic Multiple Choice Q&A on Interactive Disk - Windows format

Accountancy
Business Law
Hotel & Catering Operations
Macro Economics / Micro Economics
Numeracy
£29.95+VAT for Disk (3½" or 5¼") and Tutor's Manual

ELM Publications, Seaton House, Kings Ripton, Huntingdon PE17 2NJ
Telephone 04873-254 or 238 Fax 04873-359

From **Tourist** **Attractions** to **Heritage Tourism**

Pat Yale

A comprehensive survey of tourist attractions - from museums to stately homes, castles, palaces and gardens, religious buildings, archaeological sites and ancient monuments, industrial and transport heritage. The Arts, wildlife & the countryside, events and the marketing and management of national and international heritage.

Book - with maps, charts & diagrams. Index .
isbn 1 85450 016 3   1991   £11.95

Tourism in the U.K.

Pat Yale

A basic introduction to the business & management of tourism specially written to cover the syllabus for BTEC National & A level courses. Comprehensive, up-to-date and written in a style appealing to young people. The author, Pat Yale, is a freelance travel writer and lecturer.

Book - isbn 1 85450 0171   £6.95 (£7.95 from 1/1/93)
320 pages, paperback   Published in September, 1992
Tutor's Manual - case studies, notes and OHPs - isbn 1 85450 094 5
Published in September, 1992   £49.00 (free with 15 books direct)

Tourism Law

Jim Corke

The first text specially written on the law relating to tourism and travel.
Designed for people who are not law specialists, & for students of hospitality, travel, recreation & leisure on courses from BTEC to degrees.
Book (large paperback) isbn 0 946139 95 4 (2nd ed. '93) £10.95
Tutor's Manual: case studies , notes, statute references - isbn 0 946139 96 2
£59.00 (free with 15 books direct)

Business & Management Books
Case Studies/General/Public Sector

Cases in Global Strategy

Alan West
Book - £9.95 (large format paperback), isbn 1 85450 012 0
Tutor's Manual of model answers and notes, with a set of OHPs on business strategy & analysis: £59.00 (free with 15+ books direct) isbn 1 85450 062 7, 1992

European Business Policy - 2nd edition

Terry Garrison
Updated and expanded edition of the popular case study book including:
Europe PLC; European Space Agency; Irish Distillers; The Channel Tunnel;
Perestroika; Siemens; Plessey; the Berlin Wall; Air Europe; Ikarus; and Pirelli.
Book - isbn 1 85450 026 0   £10.95   1991
Tutor's Manual - isbn 1 85450 036 8   £59.00

Case Studies in Employment Law

Jeff Young
17 case studies on topical and typical employment law issues and problems - from unfair dismissal to reductions in wages, from maternity rights to changes of job.
Book - £7.95   isbn 1 85450 047 3   Paperback   10/1992
Tutor's Manual - isbn 1 85450 078 8   £59.00 (free with 15+ books direct)

Case Studies in Business Law

Jeff Young
20 varied and interesting case studies, designed to appeal to students studying law on the first stage of business and professional courses. Tutors without a legal background will find each case versatile (for adapting to different courses).
Book - isbn 0 946139 98 9   £6.95
Tutor's Manual - isbn 0 946139 93 8   £59.00 (free with 15+ books direct)

Case Studies in Management - Introductory level - 3rd edition

Don Parsons & Steve Millard
Enlarged and updated edition with new case studies arranged into Mini (incident studies), Midi (medium-length) and Cross-functional (longer) sections.
Book - isbn 1 85450 077 5   £7.95
Tutor's Manual - Model answers, notes, OHPs - isbn 1 85450 076 7   £49.00

Case Studies in Business Law - isbn 0 946139 98 9
Jeff Young
Tutor's Manual - worked answers, notes, relevant
statutes, OHPs - isbn 0 946139 93 8

Case Studies in Employment Law - isbn 1 85450 047 3 -
Jeff Young
Tutor's Manual - worked answers, relevant statutes,
notes & OHPs - isbn 1 85450 067 8

Exercises in Business Law - Tutor's Manual
isbn 185450 093 7
Fiona Golby
A variety of user-friendly exercises, puzzles and materials for
first level post-experience students, carrying copying rights

Business Law - interactive computer disk diagnostic
questions/answers
Editor: Humphrey Shaw
Manual = isbn 1 85450 54 7

Tourism Law - isbn 0 946139 95 4
Jim Corke
Tutor's Manual - tested exercises and cases, notes and
extracts isbn 0 946139 96 2

ELM Publications, Seaton House, Kings Ripton, Huntingdon PE17 2NJ
Tel 04873-254 or 04873-238 Fax 04873-359